TOM PAINE: FREEDOM'S APOSTLE

BOOKS BY LEO GURKO

TOM PAINE

FREEDOM'S APOSTLE

BY

LEO GURKO

ILLUSTRATED BY FRITZ KREDEL

THOMAS Y. CROWELL COMPANY

NEW YORK

For STEVE and JANE,
my own younger readers

CONTENTS

TOM PAINE: FREEDOM'S APOSTLE

LONG RETREAT

IT WAS September 1776, and by the flickering light of an army campfire a man sat on a hogshead, writing. He looked up occasionally and exchanged a word with some restless soldier drifting past. But even then his alert, slightly prominent blue eyes never lost their look of deep concentration. These, together with his large fleshy nose, the rugged set of his face and his body dressed in the rough homespun of the Continental militia, made him an impressive figure as he sat hunched over the paper poised on his knee.

TOM PAINE

His name was Tom Paine. The army of which he was a part belonged to General Washington, and for some weeks had retreated steadily before the British across the New Jersey meadows. They were now bedded down for the night on the outskirts of Newark, tired, discouraged, painfully conscious that with daybreak their retreat would continue. The war, indeed, was going badly for the Colonists. There were many, even among the soldiers, who were arguing that the whole thing was a mistake, that if the Americans would throw away their arms and go back to their peaceful pursuits, the British would overlook the rebellion and declare a general amnesty. There was growing rejoicing among the Loyalists, who had insisted all along that the Colonies were too weak to defeat the mother country and that their grievances against England could be settled through peaceful negotiation.

All these things were passing through the mind of the man writing by the fire. Until the year before, the name of Thomas Paine was totally unknown to the world. But then he had published his pamphlet *Common Sense*, arguing that the break with England had to be absolute and that a resort to armed revolution was the only way to bring it about. *Common Sense* sold by the hundreds of thousands, and its simple, logical, hard-hitting prose had been a powerful factor in driving public opinion to a final rupture with the British. Now Tom Paine was not only a household word in the Colonies from Massachusetts to the Carolinas, but a name that aroused violent feelings three thousand miles away in England.

His pen scratched on over the foolscap, and so absorbed was he in his task that he was unaware of the tall, high-booted man who had paused beside him. When the pen stopped momentarily, the man allowed his hand to drop on Paine's shoulder.

"Mr. Paine," he said. He had a slow, grave voice with a slight halt in it.

Tom looked up, then rose to his feet.

"General Washington."

"I didn't mean to interrupt your writing, and I won't keep you from it but a minute. It's just that I'm checking on our supplies, and you're one of our chief sources. Words, not bullets." The General's grave voice was edged with humor, then it resumed its normally serious tone. "As things stand now, maybe words are more important. God knows we haven't many bullets left. And at the rate these Jersey and Pennsylvania volunteers are going back to their farms, we won't have many men left by the end of the week, either."

"You're not discouraged, are you, General?"

Washington looked intently at the strongly defined features of the man before him.

"No, I suppose not. And that makes two of us, doesn't it, Mr. Paine?"

[3]

Paine smiled. The smile didn't exactly light up his face, but it softened its sharp lines.

"May I see what you've written?" The two men walked closer to the fire, and Paine handed the foolscap to Washington. The tall man from Virginia tilted the sheets toward the fire and read, his lips moving silently with the words:

> These are the times that try men's souls. The summer soldier and the sunshine patriot, will, in this crisis, shrink from the service of their country; but he that stands it *now*, deserves the love and thanks of man and woman.

"Summer soldier, sunshine patriot," the General repeated. "You write eloquently, Mr. Paine."

Paine bowed in acknowledgment.

"Let me have a copy when you finish. I have a feeling I shall have use for it before this campaign is over."

Paine bowed again as Washington, returning to his tent, was swallowed up in the darkness. Gradually a silence fell over the camp as the men dropped off to sleep, but Paine continued to labor over what was to be the first of the *Crisis* papers:

> Tyranny, like hell, is not easily conquered; yet we have this consolation with us, that the harder the conflict, the more glorious the triumph. What we obtain too cheap, we esteem too lightly; it is dearness

that gives everything its value. Heaven knows how to put a proper price upon its goods; and it would be strange indeed if so celestial an article as FREE-DOM, should not be highly rated.

Men were later to wonder how Tom Paine, the son of a humble staymaker in the small English village of Thet-ford, had come to write so well, in a style that combined so much clarity and power. His formal education had not gone beyond elementary school. He did no serious writing until his late thirties, and then only to draw up a petition to Parliament on the grievances of the excise-men. Yet, at thirty-eight, he wrote *Common Sense,* which turned the English-speaking world upside down. When asked about this sudden talent, Paine himself said he could not explain it, that it was something he was apparently born to do. If it hadn't come out until this late in life it was for lack of the right circumstances. Still, he had some acquaintance with the works of Swift, Addi-son, Dr. Johnson, among other prose masters of the eighteenth century, and their influence must have been strong.

The night was now almost completely still. Even the occasional volleys of skirmishers and outposts had died away, as the army of General Howe, a short distance to the east, had bedded down. The chill of autumn was in the air, and a layer of cloud blacked out stars and moon. To all this, the man writing by the fire was oblivious.

Britain, with an army to enforce her tyranny, has declared that she has a right (*not only* to TAX) 'BUT TO BIND *us in* ALL CASES WHATSO-EVER,' and if being bound in *that manner* is not slavery, then there is not such a thing as slavery upon earth. Even the expression is impious; for so un-limited a power can belong only to God.

It was ironic that a man whose writings were filled with so many references to God should be accused by his enemies of being an atheist—an especially damning indictment in those days. Yet the accusation persisted and became part of the Tom Paine legend. A century later Theodore Roosevelt was to refer to Paine as a "dirty little atheist," an epithet wrong on all three counts. He was no dirtier than the average man of his time. Far from being little, he was taller than T. R. And he proclaimed his belief in God on dozens of occasions, not perhaps the God of the Old or New Testament, but the God he saw every day in the world of Nature around him.

The pen stopped scratching at last. Paine rose slowly, stretched his cramped and aching muscles, put the writing away in his knapsack, and with a sigh of relief lay down on his bedroll. In a moment, he was asleep, with the opening paragraphs of *Crisis 1*, that was to electrify the young nation as *Common Sense* had done on the eve of hostilities, resting a few feet away.

The next morning, gray and chill, the army resumed

its slow retreat across the flatlands of New Jersey toward Princeton. The weather was in keeping with the mood of the men. "A good thing for us," thought Paine, trudging with the foot soldiers on the dusty highway, "the British fight such a leisurely war. If they attacked at night, that would be the end of us." He shuddered at the prospect. Being an Englishman himself, he knew the habits of his countrymen. As soldiers they slept late and retired early. Ambushes and night attacks they regarded as barbarous and savage, tactics worthy of Indians but not of civilized white men. They fought in tightly closed ranks, effective enough against the massed armies of Europe, but sitting ducks for the dispersed sharpshooters of the Colonies. And their red coats, while beautiful to look at, made perfect targets in the clear air of the New World. The Englishman was as brave a fighting man as existed, but he was a fish out of water in America. As much as anything else, it was this weakness that sustained Paine in his belief that the Americans would be victorious even in the present dark time when their cause seemed hopeless.

When Paine had joined the army at Fort Lee, Washington had offered him a mount, and invited him to ride with his staff. He got along well with Washington's staff officers, and with one of them, Colonel Alexander Hamilton, he had had some sharp discussions. Hamilton was in favor of the uprising but he wanted an independent America governed by the propertied and educated classes. This theory of a "limited" revolution was repugnant to Paine, who regarded it as no great improvement over rule by one man. Between rule by one man (the king) or rule by the whole people, there seemed to him no acceptable middle ground. Since the first had become intolerable, he was wholeheartedly committed to the second. Paine enjoyed contact with Hamilton's alert and incisive mind; his own always felt fresher and more alert afterward. Washington, by contrast, was a man of few ideas and even fewer words. But there exuded from him a power and magnetism that made him dominate whatever company he was in. If ever there was a natural leader of men, it was Washington. Even his silence was impressive.

Yet it was on the ground, among the grumbling riflemen, that Paine felt most at home. He delighted in the colloquial speech of the common soldier. The strange motley of New Jersey farmers, woodsmen from western Pennsylvania, and artisans from Philadelphia and New York was a human leavening such as he had not seen in his native England. From them, as much as from the evidence of his own senses, he learned what the New World was like: the richness of the farms, the lush forests crowded with wild game, the fertile greenness of mountain and plain. It was a country overflowing with milk and honey, richer beyond compare than the ancient Canaan which God finally permitted the Israelites to enter after their wanderings in the desert.

No wonder the Colonists resented British rule, and even the petty tyrannies of the English government seemed intolerable. It was not only that they had rich land to fight for, but that the great generous spaces of America bred in them an overwhelming desire to be their own men, beholden to no one. Sam Adams of Boston, Robert Morris of Philadelphia, and the other enterprising merchants of the large cities were against the British because of the restrictions put on the trade of the Colonies, but the farmers and woodsmen who filled the ranks of Washington's army were moved by the pure dream of independence. And it was the purity of this dream—of a society where every man was his own master—that stirred Paine to his writing, that in his mind marked off the New World from the Old, that gave his eighteen months of life in America a meaning which he had never felt during his first thirty-seven years in England.

They grumbled and swore as soldiers always do, only this time with special reason. This first campaign had been so far an unbroken succession of defeats. They had been chased from Long Island, driven out of Manhattan, and forced across the Hudson. The British seemed to have an endless supply of men and enough ammunition to equip a half-dozen armies. Their ships plied the ocean and the rivers without interference, outflanking the Americans time and again, landing reinforcements at will. For some time now, American bullets had been strictly rationed, and though they took a heavy toll of the closely packed English ranks, these filled up almost at once, and the retreat continued. At periodic intervals, whole squads of men left for home, their enlistment periods up, while those who remained behind began counting the days to the end of theirs. The new volunteers were not due to appear until after the harvest season.

September 1776 was a grim month, for the uniforms of the soldiers had grown tattered and afforded little protection from the nights that had suddenly become chill. The grumblings, the murmurs of discontent increased. "These are the times that try men's souls," cried Paine in that bitter season. Slogging along with the retreating and bedraggled army, its morale heaving visibly toward the breaking point, he stubbornly refused to believe the war was lost. America was too large, too fair, too heavily favored by Nature, by God, not to survive the ordeal of her birth. It meant too much to her, and not enough to the British. The British had overwhelming power, but they were using it lazily; they did not care enough, and because they did not care enough, they would lose. This seemed as logical to Paine as Euclid's theorems to a mathematician. He believed in the inevitability of an independent America even before he could demonstrate it as a fact.

September came to an end at last, and the slow retreat dragged into October. As the nights grew longer, the tempo of the campaign slowed, but the lessening pressure of the enemy was more than made up by the increasing cold. One afternoon, outside of Princeton, the Americans counterattacked. The British reeled back momentarily, taken by surprise, but Washington did not follow up the advantage. He could not. He was low on men and lower on ammunition. The move was designed to bolster the morale of the Colonials and to show the British they still carried a sting. For two wild hours, Paine charged with his companions, fired his musket, reloaded, fired, over and over until the gun was a live coal in his hands. Then the bugle sounded, calling them back. That night, in Princeton, exhausted by their efforts, they slept like dead men.

The next day the retreat resumed. In the long evenings, Paine would struggle over his new pamphlet, his fingers sometimes so blue with cold he could hardly grip the quill, and though he was used to writing fast, days would pass when not a word came out. The fatigue and discouragements of a losing campaign at times numbed his mind. So the motley army, its ranks constantly changing with enlistment periods ending and beginning, plodded backward toward Trenton under slow enemy pressure. There were moments when one violent, heavily muscled assault by the British would have destroyed it altogether and ended the uprising with a single stroke. The assault never came. The Colonial army wavered, bent, thinned down during one crucial week to four thousand men (General Howe never had fewer than twenty thousand, all of them well armed and well fed), seemed at several points on the verge of disintegrating altogether. It never quite did.

When it reached Trenton, somehow still intact, the first *Crisis* paper was finished. Bidding farewell to his unit and to General Washington, Paine hurried off to Philadelphia to get it printed.

"Mind you send me as many copies as you can spare, Mr. Paine," said Washington when he came to take his leave.

"I promise you that, General. And by as fast a courier as we can find in Philadelphia," Paine replied.

The two men shook hands, wished each other Godspeed, and Paine, on horse this time, took off on his southward journey.

Three weeks later, the first copies of *Crisis I* rolled off the press, and Paine with his own hands tied up bundles of the pamphlet, still ink-wet, and dispatched them to the front. They arrived two days before Christmas. A week before, Washington's army had been driven out of Trenton and over the Delaware, while the British, reinforced now by three thousand Hessian mercenaries, were settled down snugly in Trenton to await the holiday season. A numbing cold gripped the area, freezing the hands of sentries, slowing down scouting parties, and bringing clashes between the two sides to a virtual standstill. The broad, swift-flowing Delaware separated the armies, giving the hard-pressed Colonials a chance to draw breath. And in this pause, a plan slowly formed in Washington's mind.

Toward dusk on December 25, he lined his men up in bunches along the river front, and there followed one of the most remarkable acts in military history. Sergeants and lieutenants, one per group, standing under the chilling sky, read to the assembled soldiers Paine's *Crisis*. The ringing and powerful words were received in an immense silence, itself more impressive than applause. Afterward, still silent, they piled into the assembled boats, and in thick night rowed across the Delaware. They fell upon the drunken and reveling Hessians, put them to rout, and drove the British out of their warm Trenton quarters into the freezing night. When they had done all the damage their numbers allowed, they set up advance posts, melted silently back to their boats, laden with British equipment and prisoners, and rowed back to their headquarters across the river.

This daring coup proved more than a stroke of military genius. It revived the morale of the American army after the long retreat from the Hudson. It was the start of Washington's first offensive campaign. It warned the British that they had on their hands not a pushover but a full-scale war. It electrified the Revolution.

When the news reached Philadelphia, it ran through the wavering city like a brushfire. Paine heard it with grim satisfaction. If his *Common Sense* had helped ignite the Revolution, his *Crisis* was a powerful factor in its first compelling victory. The Americans had passed through the first stage of the crisis that tries men's souls—and survived.

PHILADELPHIA

Paine's first view of America was from a sickbed. He had contracted fever on the voyage from England late in 1774, and when the vessel docked in Philadelphia, he lay in his berth, his cheeks sunken, his mind dull, gazing hollow-eyed at the dismal, windowless walls of the ship's steerage.

He was among the humblest of immigrants. His purse contained no money and his entire wardrobe consisted of the clothes on his back. Though as a boy he had helped his father at staymaking, there was no trade at which he was really skilled. For seven years, off and on, he was an exciseman in the King's service, collecting taxes on com-

mercial goods. Then for a brief time he helped his second
wife run the pub she had inherited from her father. There
was no question of his following either line in the Colonies. He had been discharged from his excise post because
of a reputation as a "troublemaker," a reputation based
on his petition to Parliament urging a raise in pay for the
excisemen. The petition was unsuccessful, and he himself
was fired soon afterward. As for pub-keeping, he had no
taste for it, and in any case it would require capital which
he did not possess.

He had, indeed, only one tangible asset, a letter of
introduction from Benjamin Franklin to Franklin's son-
in-law Richard Bache, a Philadelphia importer with a
well-established business. A dozen times during the two
months at sea Paine had run his eye over this letter:

> The bearer, Mr. Thomas Paine, is very well recom-
> mended to me as an ingenious, worthy young man.
> He goes to Pennsylvania with the view to settling
> there. I request you to give him your best advice
> and countenance. . . . If you can put him in the
> way of obtaining employment . . . so that he may
> procure a subsistence at least, till he can make ac-
> quaintance and obtain a knowledge of the country,
> you will do well, and much oblige your affectionate
> father.

He was looking for employment but at what he did
not know. He had rather enjoyed writing the excise pe-

tition, and remembered telling Mr. Franklin so. When the idea of settling in America first came to him, he had gone to see Franklin, then in London on business for the Colonies, because he was the one American whom everyone in England had heard of.

Franklin could not have been kinder or more friendly. He had been informed of the excise petition, and felt that Paine would have no difficulty making his way in America.

"It's a growing country, Mr. Paine," he said, "and it needs new men badly. You look vigorous enough, and as there doesn't seem to be a future for you here, it's very sensible to think of emigrating. But I must warn you that there's trouble brewing in the Colonies over relations with England. It might quiet down or it might develop into something serious. Nobody can tell yet."

"I'm used to trouble," the Englishman replied. "Anyway, I'm in so much of it now that America is bound to be an improvement."

They talked for a while about trouble. Franklin, more than thirty years older than Paine, was a practical philosopher, and the subject of trouble was one of his favorite topics. He had given much advice on how to bear it in his *Poor Richard's Almanac,* and in his good-humored, even-tempered way, his large sleepy eyes twinkling, he counseled Paine. The conversation then shifted to the disturbances in America. This was the first Paine had heard about them, because the London newspapers were giving them little space. He listened with growing absorption as Franklin described the restrictions on trade, the taxation without representation, the oppressive behavior of many Crown agents. There was talk of civil disobedience, and even resort to arms.

"My mission in London, in fact, is concerned with getting these matters peacefully settled."

"And are you succeeding, sir?"

"Not as much as I had hoped. However, don't let that discourage you. No matter how disturbed they get, the Colonies are God's country. Everyone gets his chance there. And so, I'm sure, will you."

Whereupon he drew up the letter of introduction.

"I'll write to let to you know how I get on, Mr. Franklin," Paine had said after expressing his warm thanks, and then left. The image of Franklin, short, stout, the face full of wrinkles and smiling wisdom, rose before him. If he was a sample of what Americans were like—. This note had sustained Paine on the slow Atlantic voyage. But the epidemic that swept the ship had laid him low, and now at the gate of a new continent and a new life he was unable to move. And there was not a soul in Philadelphia even aware of his existence.

For two days the captain debated what to do with his sick passenger, but when he heard of the letter from Franklin he persuaded a doctor in town to remove Paine to his house for care and convalescence. Paine's first three weeks in America were passed in a pleasant bedroom where the doctor and, later, Richard Bache visited him regularly until he recovered sufficiently to find his own lodgings and begin this new life under his own steam. He was acutely conscious of how much he owed to Frankin, and what a magic name that was in the Colonies. Or at any rate in Philadelphia. Paine was more than ever determined that Franklin should hear only well of him.

The Philadelphia which greeted him upon his recovery was in many ways different from the cities he had known in England. It had more space and fewer slums. The streets were wider, and had paved strips to walk on— very useful when it rained and the roadways became masses of mud. The town had its poor, but they were not like the sodden creatures of London, taking refuge from their miseries in gin and lying drunk, women and children as well as men, in the gutters. The town fathers were always encouraging Philadelphia's needier residents to move westward toward the border country where land was cheap and it was easy to make a new start.

Philadelphia had inns, pubs and coffeehouses, as did London, but they catered to a wider clientele, and men from many different walks of life rubbed elbows there. Differences in station were apparent enough in the way people dressed, but these were not as marked nor as wide as in England. The town was a Quaker city, and though its movements and traffic were no less animated, its coloration was more subdued and its inhabitants, in the spirit of their religious beliefs, were quietly friendly, hospitable and pacific. Paine's father had been a Quaker and had brought up his son in the Quaker spirit. In no American city could he have felt more immediately at home.

Though Philadelphia was the largest community in the Colonies, its population scarcely exceeded thirty thousand. Paine found it a great contrast with London, whose population was ten times as large. And the contrast seemed to him all in favor of the City of Brotherly Love, as it was already called.

On the recommendation of Richard Bache, he went to see a printer and bookseller named Robert Aitken, who published a monthly periodical called the *Pennsylvania Magazine*. The editorship was vacant and Paine was offered the job, which he kept until the middle of 1775. As editor, he inclined toward daring themes and developed a hard-hitting style. He wrote articles poking fun at dueling, attacking slavery, defending the rights of women. With trouble in the air between the Colonies and Britain, Paine took an increasing interest in politics. He began his editorship believing in conciliation and wound up advocating an outright break.

For this change of heart, two things were responsible. One was the vigor of the Colonies, which poured out of the very streets. Woodsmen, mountain men, trappers, sturdy farmers, dressed every which way, streamed through Philadelphia. They all had a confident, even cocky air. They held their heads high and looked boldly at the world around them. Paine drank with them in taverns, talked with them about their families and land and their feelings about independence, found lodgings for them when the inns were full. They gave him an early vision of what America was like, her size, strength, sweep, and sheer overwhelming energy. That such a country should be tied hand and foot to a tiny island like Britain seemed to Paine increasingly grotesque. He was soon to write in *Common Sense:*

> . . . there is something absurd, in supposing a continent to be perpetually governed by an island. In no instance hath Nature made the satellite larger than the primary planet; and as England and America, with respect to each other, reverse the common order of Nature, it is evident that they belong to different systems: England to Europe—America to itself.

An even stronger factor in Paine's change of view was the unyielding attitude of the British. Their attitude toward the Colonies was that of a stern father toward an unruly child. George III took every American petition as a personal affront. His ministers looked upon the Colonies as strategic pawns in the wars against the French. Most influential Englishmen thought of the overseas possessions of the Empire as dumping grounds for slaves, convicts, and indentured servants, or as places where propertyless young men might make quick fortunes. The wealth of the Colonies was exploited for all it was worth. American businessmen were not allowed to compete with their British counterparts, and American trade with other countries had to be processed through British ports and handled by British agents. A staggering amount of money poured from America into the pockets of English politicians, middlemen, landlords, investors, and into the Crown treasury itself.

The attempts of the Colonies to redress their grievances, to loosen the iron clamp of the mother country, were met by a policy alternating between duplicity and force. At times the British authorities greeted petitions with courtesy and a show of reason but with no intention of doing anything about them. At other times petitions were rejected brusquely and the offending Colony threatened with reprisals. Voices were raised even in England against the treatment of the Colonies. The most eloquent was that of the celebrated orator Edmund Burke, who declaimed in Parliament on the folly of a system that could have only one result: driving the Colonials to open and perhaps successful rebellion. This seemed absurdly improbable to his fellow M.P.'s, who believed that, even if it came to the worst, the overwhelming military power of Britain would make any uprising short-lived.

So matters stood at the beginning of 1775.

Then came the event which, for Paine at least, settled the whole question of peace or war. The British sent an army marching through the countryside outside Boston to intimidate the inhabitants, and thereby touched off the Battle of Lexington. The shots of that historic skirmish, the first armed clash between the Colonies and the mother country, may have been heard around the world. More to the point, they were heard in Philadelphia. The news sent the Continental Congress, meeting in that city, into a frenzy of excitement and convinced many moderates that perhaps everything had been taken out of their hands, and that now the die was irrevocably cast. Philadelphia was thrown into a turmoil of debate on the great question of the hour. And wherever the argument was hottest, there was Paine, poking his inquisitive nose into knots of arguing men, soaking up public opinion as befitted a good editor, but also making up his own mind in the process. When word came of the Battle of Bunker Hill, the discussions grew even more feverish and there was talk of raising volunteers for the relief of Boston.

Yet the prominent men in the Congress, Thomas Jefferson among them, refused to entertain the idea of war. The idea was too new, too unthinkable. Ties with England, sentimental as well as political, were too strong. Through the spring and summer the argument over what to do next raged on, splitting the city into factions, often

cutting across family lines. Many of the older Philadelphia families were staunchly Loyalist and were to remain
so throughout the long war. But within even their ranks,
the younger members were beginning to be drawn
toward the idea of rebellion and independence. If a poll
had been taken at midpoint that year, a majority would
in all probability have declared in favor of conciliation.
The margin would not, however, have been great. The
whole issue hung delicately in the balance. One strong
push in either direction would be enough to tip the
scale.

As for Paine, he had never felt so alive or excited. At
last he had found a movement, a cause, a country, he
could throw himself into. The sense of being in at the
birth of something new came to him very strongly. He
talked and argued in the taverns till all hours, worked
furiously at articles and editorials for his magazine, in-
terviewed the leaders of the Continental Congress, and
began quarreling with his boss. Aitken was a man of
strong conservative views, from timidity as much as
from conviction. He did not want trouble, he did not
wish to offend the "best" people, who were, after all, still
loyal to the Crown. Yet he was a businessman anxious to
make a profit. When Paine took over the *Pennsylvania
Magazine*, it was dying on its feet. In six months its circulation had tripled and it had become a paying proposition.
This was due largely to the writing of its firebrand edi-

tor. Many of Paine's ideas were daring and new, and were written in a sharp, lively, stinging style. To Aitken they seemed very radical, but his cautionings had no effect on Paine. For several months the publisher wavered between conviction and profit. Finally, conviction won, and Paine and the *Pennsylvania Magazine* parted company.

The hitch as editor did three things for Paine: he saved enough money to live for a while without working; it made him a well-known figure in Philadelphia; it gave him a chance to serve his apprenticeship as a writer. With the money saved he was freed for a time from job-hunting. The contacts he had made enabled him to remain in close touch with the influential men on the Colonial side. The apprenticeship prepared him for the writing of the pamphlet that was to catapult the name of Thomas Paine into history.

Convinced now that the British were unyielding, his own mind made up about the need for an outright break, Paine plunged into the writing of *Common Sense*. If fame is as much a matter of timing as talent, the timing for the appearance of such a work could not have been more perfect. The Colonies were seething with indecision. There were small armed clashes between the British and hastily assembled local forces, though this skirmishing in itself was not serious enough to be called open war. The splitting of public opinion was almost certain to maintain the uneasy status quo in which the British would grow stronger and the Americans, in relation to them, weaker.

Into this feverish caldron of agitated public opinion, Paine plunged with both feet. For the first time in his thirty-eight years, his life had acquired an exhilarating meaning and purpose. He was part of a large and as yet unformed human mass. He would help to form it. With this resolve, he began work on *Common Sense*. Within three months, September, October, and November of 1775, working in his room by day, refreshing and re-newing himself in the pubs and coffeehouses by night, he had finished the epoch-making pamphlet.

In it, he ridiculed the King:

> In England a king hath little more to do than to make war and give away places; which, in plain terms, is to impoverish the nation and set it together by the ears. A pretty business indeed for a man to be allowed eight hundred thousand sterling a year for, and worshipped into the bargain!

And argued against the solidity of America's tie to Britain:

> I have heard it asserted by some, that as America has flourished under her former connexion with Great Britain, the same connexion is necessary towards her future happiness, and will always have the same effect. Nothing can be more fallacious than this kind of argument. We may as well assert that because a

child has thrived upon milk, that it is never to have meat, or that the first twenty years of our lives is to become a precedent for the next twenty.

And reasoned that Britain was not equipped to handle the affairs of America:

> As to government matters, it is not in the power of Britain to do this continent justice: the business of it will soon be too weighty and intricate to be managed with any tolerable degree of convenience, by a power so distant from us, and so very ignorant of us. . . . To be always running three or four thousand miles with a tale or a petition, waiting four or five months for an answer, which, when obtained, required five or six more to explain it in, will in a few years be looked upon as folly and childishness— there was a time when it was proper, and there is a proper time for it to cease.

And urged that the time for independence was now:

> Youth is the seed-time of good habits, as well in nations as in individuals. It might be difficult, if not impossible, to form the continent into one government half a century hence. The vast variety of interests, occasioned by an increase of trade and population, would create confusion. Colony would be against colony. Each being able, might scorn each other's resistance: and while the proud and foolish gloried in their little distinctions, the wise would lament that the union had not been formed before. Wherefore the *present* time is the *true time* for

establishing it. The intimacy which is contracted in infancy, and the friendship which is formed in misfortune, are, of all others, the most lasting and unalterable.

And invoked the epic birth of a new nation:

We have it in our power to begin the world over again. A situation, similar to the present, hath not happened since the days of Noah until now. The birthday of a new world is at hand, and a race of men, perhaps as numerous as all Europe contains, are to receive their portion of freedom from the events of a few months.

Though *Common Sense* was a masterpiece of reasoned argument, Paine had no illusions about the powers of persuasion alone. "Time," he wrote in the Introduction, "makes more converts than reason." He believed, and asserted over and over, that in the end the truth would prevail.

After the pamphlet was written, the search for a printer began. This was harder in those days than now. There were plenty of printers, but few who were willing to take a chance on a work so explosive. Paine did not even attach his own name to it; *Common Sense*, when it did come out, was simply signed AN ENGLISHMAN. A printer named Bell finally expressed willingness to bring it out, but in view of the special risks involved, he demanded no less than half the profits. Paine did not haggle. He not only agreed to Bell's terms, but insisted on turning over his own share of the proceeds to the revolutionary cause. More than a hundred thousand copies of *Common Sense* were sold within the first three months alone. Bundles were shipped to every large town in the Colonies and hawked through the streets by newsboys. Nearly everyone profited from it except the author.

Throughout his life, Paine's attitude toward money was foolish and inconsistent. He refused to benefit from the sale of his works, yet was always complaining that the Congress or the Colonial legislatures were slow to reward him for his services in the war. Often he was hard up for funds as a result of his own perversity, and would then demand that the government support him. He made a nuisance of himself to his friends and public sponsors by dunning them for state pensions or jobs, while turning up his nose at a reasonable return from the fabulous sale of his own writings. He spurned legitimate royalties because of the principle that an author should not personally profit from works devoted to the welfare of mankind. He insisted on government support on the principle that men who devote themselves (even unofficially) to the service of a government ought to be rewarded by it. While doing everything on the basis of principle, he managed to be the greatest financial irritant to his friends and associates.

In 1782—under pressure from Paine—Washington, Robert Morris and Robert Livingston wrote to Congress that Paine had been "of considerable utility to the common cause by several of his Publications." Congress postponed their request that Paine be given an income. But they managed to secure for him a salary of eight hundred dollars a year from special government funds that he might continue to use his "abilities" in "informing the People and rousing them into action." Yet two years earlier, Paine had spent the last five hundred dollars of his own money to start a fund in the Pennsylvania Assembly (of which he was clerk) in answer to Washington's appeal for aid to his troops. No wonder that at the end of the Revolution he was without money again. He was moved to remark:

> I cannot help viewing my situation as singularly inconvenient. Trade I do not understand. Land I have none, or what is equal to none. I have exiled myself from one country without making a home of another; and I cannot help sometimes asking myself, what am I better off than a refugee . . . from the country I have obliged and served, to that which can owe me no good will.

Responding to his cries of injustice, Pennsylvania gave him five hundred pounds in cash and New York bestowed upon him a confiscated Loyalist farm in New Rochelle. In material ways he was generously treated by the grateful American Colonies. His troubles need never have arisen had he displayed ordinary common sense in the publication of his own works. One of the contradictions in Paine was his hard-headed logic and clarity in the political arguments of his pamphlets, and the soft-headed muddle and foolishness he displayed in money matters.

Common Sense came out in January 1776. Its effect was that of a lighted match dropped in a sea of oil. Public opinion was not only strongly divided on the subject of relations with England, but evenly divided as well. British troops were continuing their sorties after they had suppressed the resistance in Boston. No policy could have been more foolish, for it kept resentment against the mother country at a high pitch when it might otherwise have died down. Into this inflamed situation came *Common Sense*. It was more than an instant success, more than a "best seller." It was a brand that spread through the Colonies like wildfire. Copies were snatched up, read (often in one hot burst), brought into taverns and coffee-houses, into private parlors and public halls, and there argued over, discussed, assailed, defended in a sudden final rush of partisan passions.

Paine's arguments for an outright break touched off the last debates and were a powerful factor, perhaps the decisive one, in driving the Colonies into the Revolutionary War. Not only were these arguments cogent, but they were expressed in a language so simple and unadorned that even the humblest folk who could read recognized it as their own. "I bring reason to your ears," he announced to his readers, "and in language as plain as A,B,C, hold up truth to your eyes." It soon became known that the man who signed himself AN ENGLISHMAN was really Thomas Paine, and with a single bound the author became one of the most renowned and popular figures in the New World. And at the same time, and for the same act, one of the most hated.

The men who disagreed with Paine and remained loyal to England recognized the power, the immense impact of his work. They made *Common Sense* the target of numerous rebuttals, and Paine the focal point of personal attacks. Charges that he was a drunkard, that he dressed in filthy clothing, that he was not a gentleman, that his friends and companions belonged to the lowest dregs of society, appeared now for the first time. Gouverneur Morris, a conservative politician who detested Paine, could not understand how "a mere adventurer from England, without fortune, without family or connections, ignorant even of grammar, could have been placed in the position he held."

These charges were to grow louder and more bitter later in his career. There was little truth in them to start with, and they grew no truer with the passage of time. But among those who wanted to believe them in the first instance, they were accepted from the outset as probably true, and later as gospel truth. When the reasoning in *Common Sense* proved too powerful to refute, the attempts to discredit the moral reputation and social standing of the author gained in force. There were more ways than one of skinning a cat even in those days, and in time Paine was to be skinned by all of them.

Common Sense swept through the Colonies, made its deep impress on the American mind, and drove public opinion toward the final break with Britain. The Continental Congress called for volunteers, appointed George Washington commander-in-chief of the first American army, and empowered a committee headed by Thomas Jefferson to draft a declaration of independence. Paine himself now rode the full crest of the tide rushing toward the war of liberation. His first leap from obscurity had come as the editor of the *Pennsylvania Magazine*. As the author of *Common Sense,* he catapulted into the front ranks of the leaders of the movement he had helped arouse.

For Paine, the spring and summer of 1776 was a time of furious activity. He went up and down Philadelphia urging the citizens to rally to the cause of independence. He traveled in the outlying areas, speaking to farmers and villagers, to travelers, backwoodsmen, men from the frontier areas of the west, urging them to volunteer for the militia. He contributed whatever money he got from

Bell to the purchase of arms, uniforms, horses, and supplies. He plunged into consultations with various leaders of the Continental Congress who called on him for advice and used him as a whetstone to sharpen their own ideas. He met Jefferson, who was to be a lifelong friend, and played a part in the hard thinking that went into the Declaration of Independence. Franklin returned from London where *Common Sense* had gone the rounds of liberal circles and roused the fury of the royalists. Paine was something more to him now than a penniless Englishman of uncertain talents whose passage to America he had in all probability paid out of his own pocket.

When they met again, with the gathering storm about to burst, with Philadelphia at its center teeming with agitation, excitement, and wild rumorings, Paine had a better coat on his back than in London, but he was otherwise unchanged. "For my own part," he had written to Franklin ruefully a short while before, "I thought it very hard to have the country set on fire about my ears almost the moment I got into it; and among other pleasures I feel in having uniformly done my duty, I feel that of not having discredited your friendship and patronage." Paine was invited to supper by Richard Bache to see Franklin on his return from Europe, and there the elderly American statesman referred to Paine's experiences.

"You know, Mr. Paine," he suggested shrewdly, "I

think you enjoy these exciting times, and wouldn't be at all pleased if things settled down to a humdrum pace."

"You may be right, sir," Paine laughed, "but there is such a thing as the times being too hectic."

"To change the subject, Mr. Paine. May I ask you something frankly? Since returning, I've heard two opinions of you. Men like Jefferson and Monroe swear by you and think you're the ablest man writing for the American cause. Others, like Gouverneur Morris, think you a low dog, say that you consort with riffraff and are only a troublemaker who will discredit whatever issue you defend." All the while Franklin was gazing at Paine intently, but the tone of his voice was, as usual, gentle and easy. "Now, Mr. Paine, what think you of these differing opinions? They can't both be right."

There was a pause. Paine had heard these sentiments already, but they had never before been put to him by so friendly a source.

"You're not obliged to answer. I ask only to satisfy my curiosity."

"But an answer you shall have. To start with, I do not think *Common Sense* discredits the cause of independence, but aids it. And aids it in no small way. As for being a low dog, greater men than I have been tarred with viler epithets with about equal cause. Mr. Morris speaks harshly of me partly because he does not like my views but principally because I am not what he considers a gentleman in the matter of birth. In this he is right. My father was a staymaker and apprenticed me to that trade. If this is a sign of inferiority, then the great majority of Americans are inferior. This I deny, and so of course would they."

"And so do I," replied Franklin. "From what I have had occasion to observe, your friends are right and your enemies wrong, and I am glad that I encouraged you to come to America. My own father, by the way, was a candlemaker, so perhaps Mr. Morris has his doubts about me, too. But I repeat what I told you in London. Our country needs devoted men for the great trial that lies ahead. Since you are plainly one of them, Mr. Paine, here is my hand on it."

And so they parted, to be caught up at once in the great trial itself. They were to meet many times before Franklin's death in 1790. To the end, their relationship never wavered from the sympathy and understanding with which it had begun.

Meanwhile, events were moving rapidly toward the ultimate break with Britain. Though skirmishing and a kind of unofficial small war had been going on for months, the issue of war and peace was still not decided. The unwillingness of the Crown to make even the mildest gestures of conciliation gave powerful support to the argument in *Common Sense* that the Colonies had everything to lose and nothing to gain under continued rule by George III. It also spurred the committee drafting a declaration of independence to get on with its work more rapidly. The declaration went through several versions in the spring. Ideas about self-government, about the inalienable rights of man, were saturating the very air of Philadelphia at that time, ideas to which Paine had already given eloquent statement. Finally, after much pulling and hauling among sectional groups in the Congress, the Declaration of Independence was adopted. Signed by Jefferson and Franklin among others, it was proclaimed on July 4, 1776. Its appearance burned all bridges leading to reconciliation with England, and on that day the Revolutionary War officially began.

Three weeks later, Paine joined the Pennsylvania volunteers under General Roberdeau, on his way to join the army of General Washington fighting for its life on the sandy plains of Long Island and in the streets of Manhattan. Thus began the campaign which, after the long and bitter retreat across New Jersey, was to produce the first of the great *Crisis* papers and the stunning rally across the Delaware River that kept the war from ending then and there.

SILAS DEANE AFFAIR

THE success of *Common Sense* and *Crisis I* brought Paine to the political forefront, and early in 1777 he was appointed Secretary to the Committee for Foreign Affairs of the Continental Congress.

This was a job of great importance, involving negotiations with foreign powers. These were often secret, which placed upon the secretary the pressing need for discretion and tact, for delicacy of feeling and absolute incorruptibility. Of these qualities, Paine was endowed only with the last.

However, he discharged his many duties conscientiously and, for a time, without incident. He continued to write *Crisis* papers as issues demanding them arose. One *Crisis* paper was addressed to the large commercial houses of the Colonies whose traditional business with England was cut off by the war. These interests were wavering in their allegiance to the American cause, and looking for ways to end the war on almost any terms. In his paper Paine argued that their short-term losses would be more than made up by the long-term gains, that under British rule American businessmen were as restricted in their freedom of action as all other Americans, and that trade could prosper freely only when independence was won. These arguments were effective. Though the British occupied Philadelphia in the fall of 1777, driving Washington's army into the terrible privations of the winter at Valley Forge, the most powerful merchants, bankers, and shippers resumed their support of the war.

As a result of this and other events, Paine grew aware that the war was not being fought on the battlefield alone. There was also the war for men's minds, to which his writings had contributed so heavily. In his new post as secretary, he now became acutely conscious of the political war that was raging just as fiercely as the military. France and England were contending for supremacy in Europe as well as in North America. The uprising of the Colonies was of great importance to France because it distracted and weakened England. The French thereby became the natural allies of the Americans. Indeed, negotiations between American agents and King Louis XVI had been going on for some time.

To Paine this was further proof of the incurable stupidity and incompetence of kings. He could understand how, in certain circumstances, one king might wish to destroy another. That a king should ally himself with a republic to undermine the principle of royalty was surely the height of madness. France and England as *countries* might be rivals for empire. Louis XVI and George III as *kings* had as their mutual interest the need to suppress republicanism. In a rational scheme of things, thought Paine, the French monarch might support the American Colonies in their struggle to be freed from England if they proposed to set up their own monarchy. But to support them in their anti-royalist sentiments, in their expressed republicanism, was a kind of suicide. It might gain the Bourbons a temporary advantage in their territorial wars with the British, but only at the price of undermining royalty as a system of government.

These observations didn't keep Paine from seeking as much French support as could be had. They simply strengthened the convictions expressed in *Common Sense* that America would be far better off without a king and removed altogether from the rivalries of Europe. France and England—those great powers—were committed to policies unworthy of their position in the world. The English refused to yield a crumb or two, and thereby were in danger of losing the whole Colonial loaf. The French royalists, unable to distinguish between their temporary and permanent enemies, were giving aid to the permanent ones in order to defeat the temporary. From these follies, Paine saw very clearly, America could only benefit. In his diplomatic efforts, he sought to extract the maximum advantages for the Colonies. When the Marquis de Lafayette arrived and enlisted in the American army, Paine welcomed his example enthusiastically and urged other individual Frenchmen to do the same. French aid, spotty and haphazard at first, increased as the war dragged on and in the end was a decisive factor at Yorktown.

King Louis was anxious to help the Americans from the start, but he was at peace with England when the Revolutionary War broke out, and he therefore could not send money and supplies openly. Instead, he encouraged French merchants to trade with the Colonies by underwriting the extension of credit to the Americans and guaranteeing the shippers against losses at the hands of the British fleet. Overseas trade continued at a brisk pace with the Colonies even after the English blockaded the coastline and began confiscating ships bound for

American ports. Goods brought much higher prices from the beleaguered Colonials than on the Continent, making America an extremely tempting market to venturesome sea captains. Moreover, individual Colonies continued to maintain, even in England itself, agents whose main task was to keep open the flow of trade. By a cruel irony, many a British soldier was killed by carbines and powder smuggled into American hands from England after the outbreak of hostilities.

Among the schemes hatched by the French government to aid the Colonies was a plan to give them a million gold *livres* as an outright gift. This could not be done officially since the British would certainly denounce it as a hostile act. It had to be done by subterfuge. One of the glittering ornaments at the court of Louis was a young and brilliant playwright, wit and gallant named Beaumarchais. He was the author of two famous comedies, *The Barber of Seville* and *The Marriage of Figaro*, on which Rossini and Mozart were later to base their celebrated operas. Beaumarchais was also an intriguer and entrepreneur with an itch for money and a flair for playing the angles. Louis appointed him agent for the transfer of the million *livres* to America.

For his part in the maneuver, Beaumarchais was paid a commission. Not content with this, he planned to spend half the gift money for powder in France, sell it for the higher price prevailing in the Colonies, and pocket the difference himself. He had other irons in the fire, too. What started out as a gift soon turned into a complicated operation for lining the pockets of Beaumarchais. Still, none of this would have greatly affected the Continental Congress and its Secretary to the Committee for Foreign Affairs had there not appeared on the scene at this point the man who was to blow up the affair into one of the famous scandals of the day. This man was Silas Deane.

Deane was in Europe to buy arms for the Colonies, receiving a commission of five per cent on each transaction. While in Paris, he got wind of the Beaumarchais venture, and presented himself to the Frenchman as a man who knew his way around America, had valuable contacts, and could get maximum prices. It seems doubtful that Deane was aware that the money was intended as a gift. If he had, it is unlikely that he would have become involved; there would have been nothing in it for him. Beaumarchais, misusing the money for his own personal benefit, would be the last man to inform anyone of King Louis' original intention, even if Louis had not already cautioned him to be discreet.

Three ships loaded with powder finally left French ports for the new world. Two were captured by British blockading vessels. The third got through to Philadelphia, and was hailed by Congress as a great boon. The rest of the gift money found its way to America as well.

In due course, Deane himself returned from Europe and presented the bill for his services to Congress. Since the volume of purchases was large, so was the bill.

By this time, rumors had reached Philadelphia that all the money had been intended as a present from the King of France and that Deane was not entitled to a commission. Paine, a bearcat on the subject of honesty, urged that representatives be sent to Paris to find out the truth of the matter. A delegation was sent, and reported privately that the money had been a gift but that the French were not prepared to admit this openly because of the delicate diplomatic situation. When this report was received, Congress split wide open between pro-Deane and anti-Deane factions, between those who wanted to pay him off on the grounds that he had performed an honest service and those who felt he was a shady character caught with his hand in the public till.

Paine was a leader of the second group and stirred up against himself the hostility of Deane's friends in Congress, headed by John Jay. On the crucial point of whether Deane knew that the money was a gift, Paine argued that whether he knew it or not did not affect the fact that it was, and any diversion of it to private hands was robbery. Deane's friends contended that Deane had speeded up the process of getting the funds and goods to the Colonies, which was, after all, his job in Europe, and that a laborer was worthy of his hire. These discussions took place in secret session and ended in a secret vote. Deane's claim was rejected.

Instead of letting the matter rest there, the infuriated agent took his case to the newspapers, and in a series of sharply worded articles denounced Congress. This attack brought the whole affair out into the open, the last place where the French wanted it to be. Even then, the matter would have subsided quickly enough if Paine had not entered the lists against Deane once again. A controversy cannot remain alive for long unless both sides join actively in it; Paine's intervention gave the matter a far greater public importance than it actually deserved. But Paine was concerned for the prestige of Congress. Even in wartime its powers were uncertain, its authority over the individual Colonies shaky. Any attack upon it would weaken its already inadequate leadership in the prosecution of the war. When Deane transferred the issue from the relatively small question of his fee to the large question of the integrity of Congress, he aroused in Paine his fierce opposition to anything which threatened the new cause. Paine, touched to the quick, abandoned discretion and secrecy, ignored considerations of tact and diplomacy, and leaped into the fray.

He was warned against this course by his Congressional friends—by Franklin and Jefferson, by Livingston, by Henry Laurens. Gérard, the French minister to the Colonies, suggested to him that the French government would be embarrassed and displeased. To no avail. Paine had only one consideration in view: defending Congress against the slanders of what seemed to him an unscrupulous and influential scoundrel. What did it matter what the French thought or the politicians thought? What did it matter if individuals were embarrassed or put out? Or when it came to that, what did his own career matter? The great thing, the sole thing, was to win the war and achieve independence. To gain that end, Paine was willing to sacrifice everything and everyone, including himself. His enemies called him an inhuman fanatic, his friends a devoted idealist. It was certainly true that principles meant more to him than people. Yet an inhuman fanatic he was not, as his role in the French Revolution fifteen years later was to demonstrate.

Public pamphleteering was Paine's natural element, and Silas Deane proved no match for him in the journalistic slugfest that followed. He denounced Deane as a crook profiting from the trials and misfortunes of his countrymen, as a rapacious moneygrubber seeking to line his pockets from any source whatever. Repulsed in his designs by a watchful Congress, Deane was now seeking to discredit that body in the eyes of the public while pretending to do so in the name of honesty and fair dealing. Paine announced that the million *livres* were an outright gift from the French King, and there was no earthly reason for Deane to profit from it.

THE SILAS DEANE AFFAIR

The controversy raged through the summer of 1778, but once the announcement of the money as a gift was formally made, Deane's claims were demolished. Battered by Paine's scornful invective, Deane at last withdrew from the scene, without dignity, without status, and without fee. Out of the affair Congress saved some money—small enough, in all truth—and a fair amount of prestige. But Paine was presently to lose his only source of income and virtually all of his personal prestige.

The moment Paine publicly disclosed the nature of King Louis' bequest, the British delivered a bitter protest to the French government in Paris. Minister Gérard in Philadelphia made official representations in Congress about the awkward position his government had been put in by the disclosures of the Secretary to the Committee for Foreign Affairs. John Jay introduced a motion to censure Paine. After a prolonged legislative hassle, the motion was defeated by the margin of one vote. Paine had not, after all, violated any law nor had he made public any official secrets. He had simply been indiscreet. But he had been indiscreet in a job where discretion was absolutely necessary. So great was the uproar, so violent the criticisms of Deane's Congressional supporters, so lukewarm the defense of his own friends, that Paine felt obliged to resign. He did not wish to be a divisive force in Congress at a time when unity was paramount to the prosecution of the war.

There is no doubt that Paine behaved nobly but no doubt, too, that he deserved to lose his job. As watchdog of the public treasury and defender of the Congressional honor, he was playing a role for which he was well qualified by nature, and doing so out of a sense of deep conviction. But complex political interests were involved in the Deane affair, which did not lend themselves to simple treatment. And here Paine's inability to make allowances, to compromise, to give way when an issue was not wholly clear, to deal with problems in terms of the human beings involved and not just in terms of abstract morality, became a serious drawback in his career as government servant. As secretary, it was his duty to be diplomatic: that is, coolly to tot up the pros and cons, the advantages and disadvantages of each act before going ahead with it. On simple matters of right and wrong, he was a superb secretary. When the two got mixed up, Paine plunged ahead like a bull in a china shop. He reduced the Silas Deane case to a simple conflict between a crook and the Colonies. By so doing, he had no trouble arguing the case for the Colonies. This ruined Deane, but at the same time it embarrassed France, the only country in the world sympathetic to the revolutionists, and it bitterly divided Congress at a time when division of any kind was dangerous. Paine either did not know this, in which case he was hardly suited for a diplomatic task, or he did not care—in which case his usefulness to

Congress was plainly over. The second appears to be true, for he expressed no surprise at the closeness of the censure vote, and resigned shortly afterward.

This side of Paine's personality comes out again in his failure to establish permanent ties with people at any time. Passionately attached to ideas and principles, he had less interest in the personal side of life. Though he met hundreds of men at one time or another, few became lifelong friends. He did not discourage friendship. He was simply not inclined toward it. While he aroused the admiration and even devotion of many, scarcely anyone grew really close to him. On the face of it, his two marriages might indicate otherwise. But the first was of brief duration, ending with the death of his wife before a year was up. And the second, though it lasted longer, ended with separation by mutual consent. Though these events took place relatively early in life, he seems to have taken little or no interest in women afterward.

This curious detachment from individual relationships carried over to Paine's failure to strike deep roots in any one country. Though an Englishman, he never developed any strong attachment to England. America roused him to great enthusiasm but it was the *idea* of a free America more than the country itself which dazzled him. After independence was won, Paine grew restless and returned to Europe. There he remained for almost fifteen years, caught up in the maelstrom of the French Revolution.

Franklin once remarked to him, "Where liberty is, there is my country," and Paine replied, "Where liberty is not, there is mine." Whatever country was struggling for independence and freedom was Paine's spiritual homeland. He was, in short, a universal man.

The price he paid for his success in dealing with men in the abstract was an inability to deal with them in the concrete. Loyalty to an ideal in all its logical purity came easily to Paine. Handling specific human beings with all their illogical contradictions came hard. These qualities seldom go together in the same man. Yet Paine's strength as a propagandist and pamphleteer lay in this very ability to get to the heart of an issue undistracted by the confusions of life.

To this day the role of Silas Deane in the tangled affair that bears his name in American history remains unclear. Whether a villain or an innocent victim of circumstances, he leaves the scene, his motives still undetermined. Ruined finally by Paine's disclosures, his prospects in the Colonies over, he drifted to England, where he became bitterly anti-American. After the end of the war, bankrupt and without friends, he disappeared from view.

The motives of the other victim of the Deane affair, Paine himself, were wholly clear from the start. Uncompromising honesty and idealism—unchallenged even by his enemies—qualified Paine for the post of secretary in the first place. His lack of discretion and self-interest made it certain that he would not keep the job for long. Compelled by his own nature to act as he did, he campaigned against Deane, knowing what the consequences might be for himself. And if he did not know, his friends gave him enough warning. When the shooting died down, Deane had disappeared altogether, and Paine was unemployed.

He resigned at the beginning of 1779. The year 1779 was a hard one for Paine, the low point of his fortunes in America. He could not get another government job. Lacking money, he kept moving to shabbier and shabbier lodgings, and his appearance, never elegant, grew seedy. His favorite exercise had always been horseback riding, but he could now no longer afford to keep a horse. He spent more and more time indoors, his digestion suffered, his health declined. Those of his friends who kept in touch with him were shocked at his condition, and tried, without much success, to rouse him from his lethargy. Even the little writing he did at this time showed a decline of energy.

The stagnation that overtook Paine overtook the war as well. Washington's army had survived the winter ordeal of 1777–78 at Valley Forge, and later in 1778 had forced the British to retreat from Philadelphia. Now the Americans were camped at White Plains, facing at a safe distance General Clinton's army comfortably berthed in New York. Nothing was happening. For three years these two armies were to remain in their respective positions, neither making a serious move against the other. The British were certainly better off. They were well housed and fed, enjoyed the attractions of city life, and were under no military pressure. The Americans, as usual, were badly housed and poorly fed, had few amusements, and, lacking the power to mount an offensive, were doomed to static boredom. British intelligence bombarded them with propaganda leaflets describing the pleasures of New York and promising them safe-conduct if they deserted. Many did.

It was an agreeable time for the British. But their own apathy, love of comfort, and inaction were in the end to contribute heavily to their losing the war. They did so little sustained fighting they finally lost the zest for it. Their discipline grew lax, their tactics slipshod, while the Americans, inured to hardship, were the tougher army in the final showdown.

Back in Philadelphia, Paine's hardships continued. One evening a group of Deane's friends, noisy and a little drunk, ran into Paine on the street and threw him into the gutter. He arose covered with filth and staggered home. On the way various citizens remarked on his appearance, and lent substance to the rumors that in his private habits he was a drunk, disorderly, and untidy man. Desperate for money, he conceived the idea of writing a history of the American Revolution, and paying his way by getting advance subscriptions. No writer was better qualified for such a task, but his ability to sell himself was as slight as his ability to sell ideas was great. At this low period of his personal reputation, subscriptions were few and the project had to be abandoned. Gérard, whose protest to Congress about Paine had led to his resignation, offered to subsidize Paine if he would slant his writings to favor the interests of France. Paine refused, though his need was acute and the offer financially tempting.

He had meanwhile become involved in a fierce struggle that broke out within the Colony of Pennsylvania between the Constitutionalists and the anti-Constitutionalists. The Assembly, spurred by the Constitutionalists, had ratified the state constitution some months before, a document that gave the vote to laborers, farmers, and frontiersmen. This was greeted with alarm by many of the merchants, lawyers, professional men, and other community leaders as a threat not simply to their interests but to good government. This dispute was forerunner to the more famous argument later between Hamilton and Jefferson as to who was fit to govern: the educated and propertied classes alone or the people as a whole. As it happened, Deane and his friends belonged to the group which favored the repeal of the constitution, while Paine, of course, was on the other side and became its symbol.

The most powerful of Deane's friends was Robert Morris, the richest merchant in Philadelphia. In March 1779 he and his supporters organized the Republican Society to repeal the constitution. The defenders of the constitution, led by Charles Willson Peale, the famous American painter, formed the Constitutional Society, and attacked the other side as scoundrels and profiteers. Pennsylvania, like the other Colonies, was suffering from those inevitable by-products of war: shortages of food, soaring prices, and profiteering by speculators. The Constitutionalists had no trouble branding their rich opponents as heartless rogues who wanted to take not only bread away from the common man but the vote as well. The state elections were scheduled for October, and the political campaign that swept the city during the summer reached extraordinary heights of bitterness and even bloodshed.

There was wrong on both sides. The Morris group was certainly involved in food hoarding and speculation. It was in favor of winning the war but it wished just the same to conduct business as usual. The Constitutionalists, in their resentment, set up a vigilante committee of inspection (of which Paine was a prominent member) that gave to itself the power to break into warehouses, examine books, haul merchants up for "trial" before them, and even to use returning companies of soldiers to enforce its orders. Violent propaganda gushed from the printing presses of both sides. Fist fights were a common occurrence. Individual leaders were assaulted by strong-arm squads unofficially organized but operating freely.

Early in October these enmities came to a boiling climax in the Fort Wilson Riot. James Wilson was a prominent figure among the anti-Constitutionalists. One day a wild crowd of Constitutionalists gathered at Byrne's Tavern on Walnut Street, marched down to Wilson's house on Third Street, and set siege to it. Wilson and several dozen of his supporters, armed to the teeth, were on guard inside. Shots were exchanged and a small battle fought, before the city militia arrived to break up the fighting. Casualties: many wounded and one dead on each side.

The following week the state elections were held, and the Constitutionalists won an overwhelming victory. Robert Morris lost his seat in the Assembly, the constitution itself was firmly established and was never again to be seriously challenged. The anti-Constitutionalists, in favor of independence from England but skeptical of letting every Tom, Dick and Harry have a voice in running the government, retired temporarily to lament what they called the "triumph of the mob." In their eyes —and they were among the most respectable and well-to-do members of the community—Paine was naturally a more disagreeable figure than ever.

The new Assembly met at the end of the year and proceeded to elect Paine as its new clerk. Cautious as political bodies usually are, it first asked Gérard whether he would object to Paine's appointment. The French minister, weary after a year of service in the turbulent Colonies and about to leave for France, offered no objection. Thus the way was cleared for Paine's return to government service. It was not as important a job as the post of secretary in Congress. But it was a job, and it brought to an end the long year of decline and stagnation through which Paine had passed. In a letter to Henry Laurens, a prominent delegate to Congress from South Carolina who had remained loyal to Paine during the prolonged wrangle with Deane, he wrote:

> As to myself, thank God, I am well and feel much pleasanter than I did— The Clerkship is not much but it is something like business and has released me from that burden of idleness, uneasiness and hopeless thinking that got so much the upper hand of me for these three or four months past.

His new work revived his spirits notably, and he plunged into it with a good deal of his old energy. Yet his thoughts often strayed back to the summer that had just passed when, ill and unattended, low in spirits and given over to unaccustomed despair, he lay on his bed wondering why fate had brought him to America. For the first time since his arrival in the new world, he was suddenly filled with memories of his early home in England, of his childhood in Thetford, and he gave himself up to sweet nostalgia for hours at a time.

THETFORD AND LONDON

A S A BOY Tom Paine dreamed of running off to sea. Thetford, the small town in Norfolk where he was born in 1737, was not far from open water; to be a cabin boy was a standard ambition for every English lad. Privateers still operated in those days, and it was possible for men—and boys—to come back from a successful expedition with a sizable share of loot.

His father, however, was a Quaker and hated fighting of any kind. He forbade Tom to join the freebooters, and on one occasion when the boy ran off to the nearest North Sea port, galloped posthaste after him and dragged him home again. Life at home was not very exciting. His father was a staymaker, a humble enough occupation, and spent all day in his little shop fitting ladies for corsets, bodices and hoop skirts. When Tom was old enough to be apprenticed, he too was on his knees taking measurements and learning how to fit strips of whalebone together. He disliked his father's trade from the start.

His family life was hardly more agreeable. His mother, eleven years older than his father, was an ill-tempered woman who felt that she had married beneath her station and never stopped reminding her husband of it. She also differed with him on religious matters. Belonging to the Church of England, she looked down upon the Quakers as an upstart sect and was always making derogatory comments about them. Whatever normal inclination Tom might have had to organized religion was seriously weakened by the theological quarrels between his parents.

He attended the Thetford Grammar School, an uncommonly good one for so small a place. His father frowned on Latin—the Quakers regarded the pagan writers with distrust—and Paine, as a result, never even learned the rudiments of that familiar ancient language known by every schoolboy in those times. As it turned out, he had no aptitude for languages anyway; he never learned to speak French even after years of residence in France. He was thus left free to concentrate on English, from which he forged the powerful instrument of his style. Though he liked to write poetry, he was more inclined from an early age to science and philosophy. The Quaker in him distrusted the senses and the imagination, and he put his poems aside with some regret as a distraction from the serious business of the world.

The England of the 1750's, which confronted Tom when he reached his teens, was scarcely an inspiring spectacle. There were great masses of poor huddled together in indescribable misery while the rich lived in fantastic luxury. There was hardly any communication between the classes; charity, social conscience, a sense of responsibility on anyone's part for the misfortunes of others, were nonexistent. The government under the Georges, and under the great prime ministers Walpole and Pitt, thought of itself as an agency to preserve order and maintain the status quo. The Established Church had grown as remote from the needs of the people as the authorities in Westminster and Windsor Palace, and there grew up in the eighteenth century an immense revivalist movement to bring the Church back to the grass roots. This movement, known as Evangelicalism, found its expression among the Methodists and Quakers. It produced a famous poet in William Cowper, and a great number of magnificent preachers and hymn writers headed by Isaac Watts, John Wesley and George Whitefield.

Corruption was a built-in part of political life. The

rotten-borough system prevailed in Parliament. Thetford, with thirty-one voters, had two seats in the House
of Commons, and Tom would witness their sale from
time to time to the highest bidders. There was a mon-
strous amount of crime in the country. The roads were
infested with highwaymen, and travel by stagecoach was
a dangerous business. So was walking in the streets after
dark. There was no regular police force. Thieves were
chased by "runners" or "thief takers," whose services
were provided by private organizations as a kind of concession let by the cities, much like hot dog and soft drink
concessions at ball parks and public picnic grounds to-
day. Such a concession earlier in the eighteenth century
was owned by Jonathan Wild, who turned out to be one
of the celebrated racketeers and outlaws of the age. When
he was finally hanged at Tyburn, his execution was witnessed by a vast, cheering crowd that turned out in
record-breaking numbers.

Any theft over six shillings was a hanging offense.
When the poor were not driven to crime, they took to
gin, and gin rows sprang up in all the cities of England.
Individual life on all but the highest levels came cheap.
Callousness toward human beings was matched by
cruelty to animals. Bear-baiting and cock-fighting were
popular sports.

To the natural idealism of youth, this society offered
little outlet. No one seemed to care, least of all those in

authority. The mass of people were largely apathetic; the men in places of power were indifferent. These conditions fired in Tom his passion for justice and reform while providing him with virtually no opportunity for expressing it in his native country.

The dullness of life in his native village, the boredom of staymaking, made Tom ache to get away. In his eighteenth year he managed, at last, to leave Thetford by running off to sea. He joined the crew of *The King of Prussia*, a privateer raiding shipping in the Atlantic sea lanes. Paine never spoke later of his experiences at sea. But he was a man who spoke little at any time of his purely personal experiences. His future adventures were to be on the field of battle and in the arena of politics, never again on the bosom of the ocean. His later life had an element of raiding in it, but against backward ideas instead of merchant ships. *The King of Prussia* beached him on the Thames estuary after one voyage; this voyage seems not to have prospered, for he landed with little money in his purse. With scarcely more than the clothes on his back, Paine, at the age of twenty, got his first glimpse of London.

It was a city of acute contrasts, and the contrasts fascinated him. Elegant streets rubbed shoulders with squalid ones. Robert Adam was beginning to build his beautiful eighteenth-century squares in neighborhoods with slums so hideous as to make those of Thetford look like the last word in comfort. The city was never still. Traffic, noise, a bursting energy pulsed through it day and night. The raw human mass, never quiet, roared through London in a way that it never had in Thetford, where everyone retired at an early hour and total silence overtook the town. Like all big cities and all country boys, London impressed Paine as a place where everything was possible, where dreams could be realized and one's fortune made. The rapid movement of everyday life suggested that nothing was fixed, that nothing need remain as it was.

But if it was fortune he was after, he did not secure it. On the contrary, he sank into the anonymous swarm of London life almost without a trace. He frequented libraries and museums, was much interested in philosophy, mathematics and astronomy, read and educated himself in these subjects. Sir Isaac Newton was then at the height of his fame. The great scientist had discovered a world which was perfectly ordered, logical and exact, where all the parts fitted together and moved like a well-oiled machine according to a set of principles which not only existed but could be completely understood by man. This universe made a deep impression on the young student. It became the basis of his later thinking, and supplied him with the two questions that lay at the bottom of his politics. Was an institution logical? Did it proceed in harmony with the laws of Nature?

Since monarchy, for example, did not stand up to either question, Paine regarded it as an illogical, unnatural monstrosity. Kings were not specially qualified to rule other men and it was therefore not logical that they should do so. Since they had originally seized power by force, they were out of line with Nature's harmonies. Thus did Paine reason along Newtonian lines, and was the true child of his century.

Meanwhile, he was keeping alive by staymaking. But times were not good in London for a young man without connections, and in 1758 he left for Dover. In Dover, he worked at his father's trade again, and the following year married a pretty young servant girl named Mary Lambert. Having two mouths to feed instead of one did not improve Paine's situation. Husband and wife moved to Margate in search of a better life, and there, after a year of marriage, Mary Lambert Paine died in childbirth. Alone once again, Paine came back to London where for a year he drifted obscurely from one temporary job to another. He worked successively in a tobacconist's shop and at a grocer's, went back to staymaking. He resumed his interest in science and attended lectures at the Royal Academy. Repelled by his father's trade, with no special talent for clerking or business, he cast about for some more permanent employment, and in this way came at last to the excise.

The excise tax, levied chiefly on beer and ale, was a

quick, easy way of replenishing the public treasury and, like all taxes imposed at the retail level, was highly unpopular. The excisemen, who collected the tax, were inevitably unpopular, too. They visited taverns, checked all deliveries of stock, and estimated how much was due the government. The pay of these tax collectors was very low, which made them inviting targets for bribes. Much of the beer was smuggled over from the Continent, where it was produced more cheaply, and the excisemen were often paid by the smugglers to look the other way. Those who did not often woke up with a knife in their backs. From any point of view the life of these tax collectors was not an easy one. Yet it had a degree of permanence. Once in the excise, a reasonably discreet man was likely to stay for life.

Paine was one of those who did not stay for life. He was discreet enough at first but luck was against him. As an exciseman, he soon learned the realities of his new job. Though he measured beer barrels faithfully and made the rounds of his beat, he blinked at some illegal shipments, gave the benefit of every doubt to the tavern-keeper, and sought to free himself personally as much as possible from the resentment aroused by the tax. His heart was quite clearly not in his work. The role of agent for His Majesty the King did not suit him well. He was too sympathetic with the poor, for one thing, and for another, did not relish the thought of risking his skin for the fifty pounds a year that he earned. Things went smoothly enough for a time until the law of averages caught up with Paine. An excise superintendent on his rounds one day discovered a large consignment of beer which Paine had failed to report. The matter could not be hushed up, and despite his pleas and promises never to be derelict in his duty again, the young man from Thetford was fired. The year was 1765. Paine was twenty-eight.

By now fairly well stocked with scientific learning, he began looking for opportunities to put it to some practical use. For some months he worked as a schoolteacher in Kensington at half his excise salary, and when this post ended he went to another elsewhere in London, and then to a third. But these jobs dried up eventually, leaving him desperate for work. As a last resort, he went back to stay-making, worked in dim shops in the obscurer London neighborhoods, and even for a time went back to Thetford and worked with his father again. He was a supreme example of the country boy who went to the big city and did not make good.

In 1767 he was advised to apply for reinstatement in the excise. Driven by extreme poverty, he began bombarding the Excise Board with flattering, servile letters begging for his job back. Since he had been discharged for neglect of duty rather than corruption, his request was not unreasonable, and in the following year he was offered a vacancy in Lewes, Sussex. This he accepted eagerly, took a room above the shop of a Quaker tobacconist named Samuel Ollive, and settled down to his new round.

The White Hart Tavern in Lewes was the meeting-place of a social club which met weekly to drink, talk, and relax. Paine joined, and soon became one of the leading figures of the group. The talk grew into discussions, the discussions into arguments, the arguments into debates. The subjects were drawn from the day's headlines —dueling, slavery, John Wilkes' quarrel with the King on the question of press censorship, the wars in Europe, Catherine the Great, Frederick the Great, and a host of other topical themes. For the first time Paine began thinking about politics and trying his hand not only at shaping his own thoughts but at persuading others that these were right. He became aware of his talent for argument. The White Hart Inn was the first formal testing ground for the future pamphleteer.

Samuel Ollive had a daughter, Elizabeth, some ten years younger than Paine. The two became friends. Elizabeth turned down several suitors in the apparent hope that Paine would propose. Ollive died in 1769, leaving his widow and daughter to struggle along with the tobacconist's shop. Paine in the meanwhile was having trouble getting along on his excise pay. He could live on it if he were very frugal, but he had developed a passion

for reading, and books on science and philosophy were
expensive. He looked around for ways of supplementing
his meager income while continuing to lodge with the
Ollives, mother and daughter. In 1771 Mrs. Ollive suggested that he join them in the tobacconist's shop as a
full-fledged business partner and, despite his earlier fail-
ures in trade, he agreed. He married Elizabeth at the
same time, though the marriage was from all accounts
more a matter of convenience than love. For the next
three years Paine devoted whatever time he could spare
from the excise to the shop. But business slowly dwindled
and the fortunes of Paine's second marriage dwindled
with it. Debts kept piling up, until in 1774 the creditors
forced the shop to close and Paine had to go into hiding
to escape debtors' prison.

The year before, he had been selected by his fellow
excisemen to write and present a petition to Parliament
asking for a raise in salary for the whole excise service.
His achievements at the White Hart Tavern were no
doubt responsible for this honor. Leaving the shop to his
wife and mother-in-law, he went up to London in 1773,
looking forward to this break in routine and even enter-
taining some hope of success. This hope was utterly
dashed. Not only did Parliament reject the petition—
nobody in power stood to gain from better pay for the
excisemen—but the excise authorities became angry with
Paine for daring to stir up "trouble." This was the second

time he had fallen into their bad graces, and they now watched him like hawks for some excuse to dismiss him again, this time for good. They could not do so simply because of the petition, for the right to petition was sacred in England since the days of the Magna Charta, and a storm of protest would have come from the liberal element. They therefore bided their time.

Their opportunity came the following spring. Paine's procedures in the excise were much as they had been when he first joined. He did not enforce the law too strictly, ignored certain violations, pursued a live-and-let-live policy. In this he was following custom. All the other excisemen were carrying on in much the same way. A supervisor, keeping a sharp eye out for violations, would have no trouble catching any of his excisemen amiss in the strict performance of their duties. What delayed matters in Paine's case was that he did not take bribes. If he had, he would in all likelihood not have had to go into the tobacconist business. Since he was not corrupt, he was harder to catch in the violation of rules, and it was not until 1774 that strong evidence turned up indicating that the taxes he was levying were well short of the legal mark. He was thereupon discharged on the spot, though, as one of Paine's biographers put it, if the English authorities had known how much trouble he would cause them in the future, they would have given him another chance in the excise.

The spring of 1774 was filled with disasters for Paine, and marked the end of his fortunes in England. In April he lost his job with the government. In May the tobacconist's shop was closed; he himself was declared a bankrupt and forced into hiding to avoid imprisonment. In June the second Mrs. Paine announced her formal separation from him. Except for the clothes he wore, all of his personal belongings—books, furniture, scientific equipment—were sold to meet the claims of his creditors. He fled Lewes for London, his prospects dimmer than ever.

In London he tried to profit from his newly acquired taste for writing by doing odd jobs for booksellers and printers. In this he was competing with all the hack writers of Grub Street. This was a street located in a wretched section of London, where literary drudges and penniless writers lived. Most of them had long experience at a game which Paine was just beginning. He did poorly, and there were days when he had nothing to eat. Hunger was a painful experience, but it did not chill his spirit or discourage his scientific interests. His contacts with Benjamin Franklin began that summer. He wrote to Franklin asking questions about electricity, and there was an exchange of letters in which the famous American experimenter discoursed on one of his favorite subjects. All this was well and good, and kept Paine mentally alive. But if a disinterested observer had been asked to pass judgment on his career in that July of 1774, he could only have arrived at the conclusion that, in the worldly sense, Paine was a complete and utter failure.

He had failed in business, been discharged from the excise, given up staymaking, abandoned the sea after a single voyage. He had not succeeded as a school-teacher and had nothing to show for his two ill-starred marriages —neither wife nor children, not even a home he could call his own. He had found no roots in Thetford and none in London. He had made the acquaintance of many men but there were none who were his close friends. He was as unattached as a human being could be. What he did have was not visible to the naked eye: energy, drive, intellectual curiosity, a strong interest in science, an undiscouraged spirit, and a whole cargo of ideas about the reorganization of society.

His London experiences after the debacle at Lewes convinced Paine finally that there was no future for him in England. His early years had been a largely fruitless scramble from one place to another, without much purpose and with no visible direction. Though in his late thirties, at a time when most men are settled in their life-work, he was not well started in anything, had found no career, and was faced with a future as blank as his past.

It was not just his inability to make a decent living but his being in bad odor with the government that clinched matters. He could never again get a public job, even a humble one, and without support from influential men, he could not hope to rise from the wretched and anonymous poverty of Grub Street. Even the great Dr. Samuel Johnson had starved there for fifteen years before the publication of his famous Dictionary rescued him.

It was natural that Paine should think of pulling up stakes and emigrating to the Colonies. Every year hundreds of Englishmen, finding life for one reason or another unsatisfactory in the old country, were moving on to the new. As a boy, Tom had read a book on Virginia and devoured the accounts of travelers in America. These early memories came back to him now and made the prospect of emigrating more attractive. Since he would be traveling light—without possessions or dependents—the task of crossing the great ocean was not as formidable as for a family. On short rations, getting nowhere rapidly, Paine worked closer and closer to the idea of trying his future overseas.

In this mood he asked Franklin for an interview. It was then that he received the blessing of the sage from Philadelphia and, equally important, the letter of introduction that gave him his first foothold in the new world.

The Paine who boarded the ship for America in September 1774 seemed an unlikely candidate to set the world on fire. From the outside he was a sturdy-looking man of slightly more than medium height. He had no distinguishing features, and it would be hard to pick him out of a crowd. But if one could have peered into his skull, it would be plain that he was bringing with him explosive goods. He had a strong distaste for established authority, and did not believe that things as they were had to endure for all time. Society in England under the rule of the King seemed to him bloated with injustice. He of course had not succeeded in it, but the amount of human misery created by it had impressed itself upon his mind long before the question of his own personal success or failure had ever arisen. He was also filled with the scientific ideas of logic. If a custom or institution was illogical, down with it. If a government did not improve the lot of its people, down with it. If kings were incompetent and expensive, down with royalty. If tradition or precedent, habit or custom, clashed with the logic of the matter, these would have to give way.

Paine was sailing to a country where all these ideas were churning in the public air. Seldom did situation and man float into the same orbit so unintentionally and with such perfect timing. Paine had come to the end of his old road and was ready for a new. So were the Colonies. Both had a feeling for the future stronger than their sense of the past. Both were suffering from an overwhelming feeling of rejection by the same source— England. The man and the yet unborn nation were natural allies in their common struggle for self-realization and a place in the sun.

If anyone had mentioned any of this to the thirty-seven-year-old immigrant, he would have blinked with astonishment. With an empty purse and half-filled stomach, with a packet of unsatisfactory memories, his main thought was of survival. He was embarking on a new life in the hope of just getting along. Though the opaqueness of the future did not allow him to see it, the voyage before him was a voyage of destiny, his own destiny and the destiny of the land he was soon to set foot upon for the first time.

THE
UNITED STATES
OF AMERICA

Paine played a triple role during the war. He was a soldier, a propagandist, and a diplomat, moving back and forth among the three activities with flexibility.

As a soldier he had marched and fought with Washington's army in the retreat across New Jersey in 1776. While he was in Philadelphia, his first *Crisis* paper had been read to the shivering troops just before the Christmas counterattack across the Delaware; his body may have been thirty miles away but his words and spirit were there.

In the spring of 1777 General Howe had packed his soldiers onto troopships and, to the amazed bewilderment of the Colonials, had sailed off into the Atlantic. He turned up later on the shore of the Chesapeake below Philadelphia and began marching northward on the capital city. Washington hurried out of New Jersey and rushed through Philadelphia to meet the new threat, but at the Battle of Brandywine was badly defeated by the British. The remnants of his army streamed back to Philadelphia. In the city itself Paine began frantically urging the authorities to make a stand and defend the capital. But the panic was on. The Continental Congress fled west to the town of York. Washington's troops, with Howe hot on their heels, did not stay in Philadelphia long enough for station identification. The city fell, unresisting, into British hands.

With Washington went Paine, a horse under him and a rifle in his hand. The two armies clashed again in a fogbank at Germantown, just outside Philadelphia. In the confusion and poor visibility the results were indecisive. To Paine, it was a nightmarish day, for he kept firing at targets he could scarcely identify, colliding with other mounted men, trying to avoid trampling on the wounded, with only the vaguest notion of what was going on. At nightfall, the two armies disengaged to lick their wounds and gather up the dead. The momentum of Howe's advance, however, was checked. His army moved back to Philadelphia while Washington retreated slowly in the growing cold of winter to Valley Forge, twenty miles westward.

In the dark time that followed, Paine commuted restlessly between the Congress at York and the battlefields. He was driven by a sense of guilt at holding down an office job while men were dying at the front. He therefore, whenever possible, threw himself eagerly, even recklessly, into the firing lines.

After the fall of Philadelphia, the Americans set up forts on both sides of the Delaware south of the city to harass the British and prevent the arrival of reinforcements. Paine was delegated by General Nathanael Greene to serve as liaison between one of these emplacements, Fort Mercer, and American military headquarters on the New Jersey side. He crossed and recrossed a dangerous strip of the Delaware carrying communications back and forth; his boat was a small, open one and came frequently under the fire of British guns. The sound of these guns aimed more or less at him was sweet music to his ears. It cooled his guilt feelings, heightened his sense of participation in the great revolutionary adventure, and lent weight to his counsels in the affairs of state.

Fort Mercer and its sister forts surrendered finally under the bombardments of the British fleet, and the sea

lanes to Philadelphia were freed from American interference. This added considerably to the comfort of
General Howe's occupying army, and made it less willing than ever to venture into the cold countryside in
pursuit of Washington encamped in frozen isolation at
Valley Forge. There were a half-dozen moments in that
winter of 1777–78 when one well-organized blow would
have destroyed Washington and wiped out all American
resistance south of New York. The blow never came.
The British, wined and dined by the Loyalist families in
Philadelphia, had no stomach for a freezing winter campaign. Their opportunity slipped away, and in the end
General Howe was summoned back to England to explain his wishy-washy tactics. He was replaced by Clinton, a tough, experienced and effective soldier. Clinton
held the northern front intact for the British until the end
of the war. It was the inept and blundering Cornwallis
who lost it in the south.

After the fall of Fort Mercer, Paine received another
dangerous assignment, the reconnoitering of English
pickets around Philadelphia. While performing this
thankless job, he volunteered to lead a patrol down the
Delaware to set fire to the British fleet—a kind of early
version of the suicide squad—but the offer was wisely
rejected by the American naval commander at Trenton.
A thirst for action consumed Paine at this time. He
wanted to be everywhere and do everything. He wanted

to win the war all by himself. The urge to victory, the passion for independence, blazed more fiercely in him than in most of the rebels, and indeed seemed to flare up to its maximum pitch whenever the war went badly for the Americans.

He was at Valley Forge several times that winter, and on each occasion his admiration for Washington deepened. So, apparently, did the General's esteem for Paine. They exchanged a number of letters, in which Washington described the critical condition of his soldiers. Paine kept urging Congress to drastically increase the flow of provisions to the half-starved, half-frozen army. He was soon to defend Washington himself against the demands of those who wanted him replaced. Throughout the long years of the war their relationship deepened. Several times Paine raised money and supplies for the army, and Washington, in turn, came to Paine's aid on the occasions when the writer, almost destitute, asked for help. They were men of different temperaments and radically different backgrounds, but the war bound them together in a way that it often does men who in ordinary life are scarcely likely to meet, or, if they do, are hardly likely to become friends.

Dangerous and frequent though Paine's military activities were, his chief service to the revolutionary cause came through his pen. With the *Crisis* papers, he turned the political pamphlet into a potent instrument for swaying men's minds. The thirteen *Crisis* papers that he wrote during the seven years of the war were a powerful factor in bringing it to a successful conclusion. They mirrored the great events and the sudden emergencies that kept springing up, and played an important role in solving them. Paine himself arranged for the printing. Copies were sold for a few pence each in all the Colonies, on street corners, in taverns and bookstalls, in public places wherever men gathered together.

The first of the *Crisis* papers, written late in 1776, was of course the famous one beginning with the words which still ring in American history, "These are the times that try men's souls." Addressed to the American people, it rallied them from the early defeats and inspired Washington's men on the eve of the Delaware crossing. The second *Crisis*, dated January 13, 1777, scarcely a month after the first, was addressed to Lord Howe. The British commander had issued a proclamation granting mercy and amnesty to the Americans if they would acknowledge the sovereignty of George III. All other issues in dispute, the proclamation stated, could be settled by negotiation. The proclamation was shrewdly timed to take advantage of the initial setbacks inflicted on the Colonials and to exploit the always powerful sentiment of making up with the mother country. In his reply, Paine assured Howe that the Americans had more courage than he gave them credit for, that they would never give up, and that therefore the British had no hope of winning the war. He mocked the British general for his failure to destroy Washington's army despite every military advantage, for his laziness as a leader, and his general inefficiency as a soldier.

Perhaps the most memorable thing about *Crisis II* was that it coined for the first time the name of the new country. "THE UNITED STATES OF AMERICA," Paine wrote, "will sound as pompously in the world or in history as the Kingdom of Great Britain." Paine not only helped in the birth of the new country. He also christened it.

Crisis III appeared midway through 1777 and was addressed to the Quakers of Philadelphia. The Quakers had just issued "a testimony of their loyalty to the English monarchy," and their religious commitment to nonviolence had made them, as an official body, opposed to the war from the start. Since Paine himself had had a Quaker upbringing, he knew the depth of these feelings at first hand and understood what a threat they were to the revolutionary cause. He began by noting that the Quakers refused to bear arms, "but the King of Britain may lay waste the world in blood and famine, and they, poor fallen souls, have nothing to say." Their condemnation of the revolutionists would be more consistent, Paine argued, if they had condemned the British use of force with equal vigor. He added that he, too, abhorred violence in any aggressive form, but that if a thief invaded his house he would do everything possible to repel him, as would most men.

He had paved the way for this argument in a forceful passage in *Crisis I:*

> My own line of reasoning is to myself as straight and clear as a ray of light. Not all the treasures of the world, so far as I believe, could have induced me to support an offensive war, for I think it murder; but if a thief breaks into my house, burns and destroys my property, and kills or threatens to kill me, or those that are in it . . . am I to suffer it? What signifies it to me, whether he who does it is a king or a common man; my countryman or not my countryman; whether it be done by an individual villain, or an army of them? If we reason to the root of things we shall find no difference . . .

From the Quakers, *Crisis III* went on to attack the Tories within the gates. Although Paine did not use the term, he was indicting what later came to be called the Fifth Column. The paper concluded with the proposal that anyone who refused to fight should be heavily taxed and that the money thus received should be used to support the patriots who were bearing arms.

The fourth *Crisis* appeared in September 1777. The Colonials had just been defeated at Brandywine, and Philadelphia was on the verge of British occupation. Another crisis had plainly been reached, calling just as plainly for another *Crisis* paper. Paine tried to rally the spirits of soldiers and civilians by arguing that the Brandywine defeat was not so serious—but with the capital about to fall and the defeated army streaming back, this argument seemed a little silly. Paine did not linger over it. He went on to explain the righteousness of the Colonial cause. "We seek not to enslave but to set a country free."

The fifth *Crisis* came out in March 1778, at the end of the terrible Valley Forge winter. Washington's enemies in Congress had been clamoring for his removal as commander-in-chief. They compared his military record since Brandywine unfavorably with that of General Gates, the hero of Saratoga, who had recently forced General Burgoyne to surrender—the Colonies' only military victory in two years. Paine's plea on behalf of Washington was eloquent and passionate. Any general, he wrote, can shine in victory. What is needed is a man who can endure and survive defeat. No one had proven himself more heroic in adversity than Washington, and no one deserved better of Congress than he. From there, Paine proceeded to the main subject of *Crisis V:* General Howe's policy of issuing counterfeit American bills for the purpose of undermining the Continental currency. This was an offense against the rules of war, and if Howe were to catch an American counterfeiting British bills he would hang him on the spot. And properly so. Paine then asked the inevitable question: Did not Howe deserve to be hanged for the same offense?

In 1778 Howe was driven out of Philadelphia by a resurgent and weather-hardened American army and pursued north toward New York. A fierce battle, in which Paine participated, was fought at Monmouth, New Jersey—as indecisive as was Germantown the year before, with both sides again emerging badly mauled. In Philadelphia, there was an outbreak of violence against Loyalist sympathizers who had collaborated with the enemy during the occupation, and two of them were publicly hanged. At this point the London government sent a commission to America promising liberal terms to the Colonies if only they would yield on the issue of independence. On October 28, 1778, Paine published *Crisis VI*, a sharp attack on the commission, which wound up with an impassioned plea for independence as the only condition that would solve the very problems which the British were now willing to give way on.

Crisis VII appeared on November 21, 1778, and was addressed to "The People of England." It explained how they came to be dragged into the war, and urged them of their own free will to grant the Colonies independence. Paine drew an analogy between the state and the family. There comes a time, he wrote, when children grow up and are ready to leave home; their parents bless them as they depart. Nations ought to behave in this same natural way. Their colonial offspring grow up and should be allowed to stand on their own feet with the blessing of the mother country. Paine disclaimed any personal benefit from his plea: "Perhaps it may be said that I live in America, and write this from interest. To this I reply, that my principle is universal. My attachment is to all the world, and not to any particular part . . ."

Crisis VIII and *Crisis IX*, together with a special number called *Crisis Extraordinary*, came out in 1780, and were devoted to bolstering American morale during the successful British campaigns in the south that year. While the northern front remained static, the British were occupying Savannah and Charleston, and moving slowly through North Carolina toward Virginia—and toward the decisive battle at Yorktown.

Crisis X, dated March 1782, dealt with taxation, an acute and unsettled problem among the Colonies. Congress was having great difficulty raising enough money to support the war effort, since it had no power to levy taxes. It was dependent on handouts or voluntary contributions from the individual Colonies. Paine urged that Congress be given the power to tax on the ground that the federal government must be strong if the future nation were to survive. The issue of taxation—a subdivision of the larger issue of the relationship between the federal government and the states—was to remain unsettled all through the 1780's, until the Constitution resolved it in the manner suggested by Paine.

Crisis XI, in May 1782, was an answer to England's latest, behind-the-scenes attempt to break the alliance between America and France. After exposing and ridiculing this maneuver, Paine asserted that England would fail to secure by guile what she had failed to achieve by force.

The twelfth *Crisis*, August 1782, was a reply to a pamphlet written by the Earl of Shelburne. The English nobleman had argued that the independence of America would mean the economic ruin of Britain. In rebuttal, Paine contended that England was being ruined not by the prospect of independence but by the war. In any case, it wasn't people like the Earl of Shelburne who were feeling the pinch—the rich were making enormous profits out of the war—but the great mass of poor who were paying the bills.

Crisis XIII, last of the famous series, appeared in April 1783, the month the Revolutionary War ended. It began on the same note and with the same phrases as *Crisis I*. "The times that tried men's souls are over, and the greatest and completest revolution the world ever knew, gloriously and happily accomplished." Paine, however, was under no illusion that the problems of the new country were over, and pleaded with his countrymen to be as united in peace as in war. He went on to glow over America's start in the world:

> Never, I say, had a country so many openings to happiness as this. Her setting out in life, like the rising of a fair morning, was unclouded and promising. Her cause was good. Her principles just and liberal. Her temper serene and firm. Her conduct regulated by the nicest steps, and everything about her wore the mark of honor. It is not every country (perhaps there is not another in the world) that can boast so fair an origin.

And to comment on his own role in the great train of events now over:

> So far as my own endeavors could go, they have all been directed to conciliate the affections, unite the interests, and draw and keep the mind of the country together; and the better to assist in this foundation work of the revolution, I have avoided all places of profit or office . . .

He ended the final *Crisis* on a personal note:

> It was the cause of America that made me an author. The force with which it struck my mind, and the dangerous condition the country appeared to me in . . . made it impossible for me, feeling as I did, to be silent: and if, in the course of more than seven years, I have rendered her any service, I have likewise added something to the reputation of literature,

by freely and disinterestedly employing it in the great cause of mankind . . .

But as the scenes of war are closed, and every man preparing for home and happier times, I therefore take my leave of the subject. I have most sincerely followed it from beginning to end, and through all its turns and windings: and whatever country I may hereafter be in, I shall always feel an honest pride at the part I have taken and acted, and a gratitude to nature and providence for putting it in my power to be of some use to mankind.

This *Crisis*, like all the others, was signed by the pen name now famous throughout the Colonies, "Common Sense."

During the war years Paine had found time to write on subjects outside the framework of the *Crisis* papers. In 1780 he published an article called *Public Good*, which contended that the western lands belonged to the nation as a whole rather than to the individual Colonies. Virginia, in particular, had laid claim to all the territory between her present borders and the Mississippi. So did Pennsylvania. Maryland, wedged between her two large neighbors, had visions of being squeezed out of existence. So had the other small Colonies. Paine foresaw an endless amount of conflict over this issue, avoidable only if the Colonies gave up their individual demands and conceded title to a federal government. Virginia was the most ambitious of the Colonies in this respect, and the most pressing in her claims. Paine's pamphlet aroused her anger, and the Virginia Assembly persistently refused to grant him honors, money or land in acknowledgment of his services to the Revolution, despite the urgings of Washington, Jefferson, and other distinguished Virginians.

He got into trouble with Rhode Island on another issue. Congress had levied a five per cent import duty on all goods arriving in the Colonies, the money to be used to purchase war supplies abroad. Rhode Island refused to collect the duty on the grounds that Congress had not the right to impose it and that prices were already sky-high. Paine wheeled into action again. In a series of letters to Rhode Island published in Philadelphia newspapers, he once more raised the principle of federal union. If Congress were not given the right to finance the war, the war might well be lost, and the individual Colonies, now so jealous of their privileges, would be squashed altogether. Paine even traveled to Providence to argue the issue on local grounds, but the Rhode Islanders gave him a chilly reception and he returned to Philadelphia, his mission unaccomplished. When in 1955 the mayor of Providence refused to allow a statue of Paine to be erected in the city because he was still a "controversial" figure, he may have been referring unintentionally to Paine's old feud with Rhode Island.

His last important work at this time was the *Letter to*

the Abbé Raynal. The Abbé Raynal was a French philosopher with a strong admiration for the British system of government. He had written a number of tracts, with a wide circulation in both Europe and America, in which he criticized the Colonies for rebelling and questioned the sincerity of their motives in the alliance with the French King. In his reply Paine suggested that no European could possibly understand the New World without living there. On the ticklish matter of the French alliance, Paine took the line that though each partner had its own motives and interests, the results of that alliance were good. As for the British system of government, Paine noted that he had grown up in England as a native-born Englishman and lived in the Colonies; his experience in both places forced him to conclude that Britain as a governing agency was far from ideal. In short, Paine applied to the philosophic observations of the Abbé Raynal the test of direct experience, and found them wanting. The *Letter* won a wide and favorable audience for Paine in Europe, giving his public reputation a dignity which his early pamphlets had not quite achieved.

The diplomatic side of Paine's career was hardly less active than the military and literary. As a diplomat he had scarcely covered himself with glory in the Silas Deane affair. Or so it seemed at the time. Later, after Deane's defection to the English, many of his supporters, headed by Robert Morris, went to Paine, congratulated him on his judgment, and regretted their defense of Deane. Still, Paine hardly had the smooth style of the professional diplomat; he was too blunt and candid, and tripped too easily over his own principles.

The first chapter in his diplomatic activities ended in 1779 when he lost his job as Secretary to the Committee for Foreign Affairs. At the end of that same year Paine's difficulties were cleared up by his appointment as clerk to the Pennsylvania Assembly, and he plunged back once again, with renewed vigor, into the pursuit of his chief aim—bringing the war to a successful conclusion. But as clerk, his diplomatic activities were more confined than his earlier work as secretary in Congress. After serving faithfully all through 1780, he grew restless and began longing for a wider outlet for his energies.

His career as clerk was marked by two major events. He wrote the first proclamation of Negro emancipation in America when an act for the abolition of slavery in Pennsylvania was introduced in the Assembly and eventually passed. He raised funds for Washington's army at a time when the General was calling desperately for help. Otherwise his duties were largely routine.

The real source of his restlessness was the stagnation of the war. The front between New York and White Plains had not changed since 1778. The morale of the Colonial army there was deteriorating steadily. Two of the regiments mutinied against bad living conditions and the boredom of inactivity; the mutiny was suppressed with great difficulty and at the cost of some lives. Meanwhile to the south, the British had landed another army which, after capturing Charleston and Savannah, was pushing north. The French fleet, dispatched from France months before to help the American cause, had not stirred from its haven at Newport for some time. The year 1780 was a bad one altogether for American military fortunes, which made men like Paine, deeply committed to an outright victory, chafe more restlessly than ever.

The key to the Colonial war effort was money. Raising enough to keep the army supplied and mobile was a headache from the beginning, and was never at any point really solved. Congress depended on handouts from the Colonies, and constantly proposed taxes which the Colonies refused to approve. The army never had enough arms or supplies to build up a reserve, so that no long-range planning was possible. The Americans had every reason for losing the war but one: the British did not want to win it badly enough. At various times, the financial situation grew so serious that only the sudden appearance of large and unexpected gifts from France kept the government from bankruptcy. The Beaumarchais "loan" in 1778 had arrived in the nick of time.

At the beginning of 1781, another such emergency was at hand. Washington had issued one of his many desperate appeals for help. Like most of the others, it fell on deaf ears. The Congressional treasury was empty. Private sources of money had virtually dried up; even the rich merchants who had previously raised funds on a voluntary basis were short of cash. As a last life-or-death resort, Congress decided to send a mission to France to ask for still another loan from King Louis. The man picked to head the mission was Colonel John Laurens, who had distinguished himself in the fighting and was the son of Henry Laurens of South Carolina, who had stood by Paine in the dispute over Silas Deane. Colonel Laurens, inexperienced in civil matters, asked Paine to accompany him. Paine leaped at the offer, resigned his clerkship, and the two men set off for France in March.

Two months later they arrived in Paris and began at once to negotiate for a loan. The sum agreed upon back home was eight million dollars, or two and a half million *livres* in French money—a huge sum for those times. Laurens turned most of the negotiations over to Paine. A soldier by training, he felt out of place and ill at ease at court, in drawing-rooms, and over conference tables. Not that Paine was to the diplomatic manner born, but he was more experienced in these affairs than Laurens. He had several audiences with King Louis, whom he seemed to have impressed favorably, and many more with Vergennes, the foreign minister. No great amount of special pleading was necessary. Keeping the Colonies from collapsing was a matter of immediate self-interest to France.

She had already invested money in the American cause, sent a fleet under De Grasse and soldiers under Rocham-beau and Lafayette. If this investment was not to be lost altogether, it was obvious that she would have to pour still more money into the coffers of Congress and keep Wash-ington's army alive.

Franklin was American minister to France in this pe-riod, and his house at Passy, a suburb of Paris, was a gathering place for many of the philosophers, scientists and writers of the day. Diderot, Condorcet, the Baron d'Holbach, with other members of the famous school of Encyclopedists as they were called—the liberal and ad-vanced thinkers of the time who were preparing the ground for the French Revolution—were friends of Franklin. He of course shared many of their ideas, and yet at the same time his warm and genial personality made him agreeable and effective in his dealings with the Crown.

Paine's reputation had preceded him in Europe, and he was made welcome at Passy as a celebrated and im-portant figure. Franklin was proud of his protégé. The differences that had sprung up between them over the Deane affair had disappeared now that Deane had broken with America, and they resumed their original relation-ship, which had something in it of master and pupil, of father and son. That spring and early summer was a time of great pleasure and intellectual stimulation for Paine.

The negotiations for the loan were moving to a successful close. He was in the company of the most brilliant and learned men of the age. He was being entertained with great warmth and hospitality, and received as a friend and equal. If not for the war and the perilous state of the revolutionary cause, if the fate of America did not hinge so directly on getting the French loan, Paine would have found it hard to leave at all.

But leave he and Laurens did, with the two and a half million *livres* in silver, filling two huge double casks. They also took with them a shipload of clothing and supplies, and the blessings of the French, royalist and republican alike. They slipped through the British blockade covering the Atlantic coast, and arrived home in August. The goods and money were a blood transfusion to the slowly dying Revolutionary cause. The half-starved soldiers wolfed down the food bought with the new silver, threw off their rags and donned fresh uniforms, replenished their empty ammunition pouches. The general staff laid plans for the next campaign.

Washington and Admiral de Grasse agreed that the immediate danger from the enemy was in the south, and drew up plans to engage the British forces under Cornwallis pushing up from Charleston. Washington pulled out of White Plains and began the long march to Virginia. De Grasse's French fleet left Newport, where it

had been at anchor for so long, and headed for Chesapeake Bay.

Back in Philadelphia, his mission successfully accomplished, Paine was once again without a job. He wrote to
Washington asking for help. It was then that Washington persuaded Robert Livingston and Robert Morris—
once Paine's enemy, but now his admirer—to do something for the unemployed patriot and pamphleteer.
Aware of the importance of Paine's pen, they secured
for him a stipend of eight hundred dollars annually for
the duration of the war, if he would continue to write
on behalf of national independence. The offer was dignified, fair, and entirely in keeping with Paine's talents.
He accepted.

The war in the South, which had begun with a series
of easy and uninterrupted victories by the British, was
moving toward an unexpected climax. The plan agreed
upon by Washington and De Grasse was to catch Cornwallis in a pincers between land and sea. They had no
very great hope it would succeed. De Grasse had first to
slip by the British fleet. Cornwallis had to be lured to do
battle in a seacoast town; if he chose to fight inland, he
could not be boxed in from the sea. There was the constant danger that the same strategy would be applied
against Washington's army. But it was the only plan that
permitted the use of the French fleet as an offensive

weapon, and the Americans, so long on the defensive, were desperate to break the long demoralizing pattern of a war that was now in its sixth indecisive year.

With the odds a hundred to one against the plan working, it worked. Everyone—particularly the British—co-operated perfectly. In the dead of night De Grasse slid into Chesapeake Bay unnoticed. Cornwallis, marching steadily northward and encountering little opposition, grew lax in his scouting. His intelligence gave him no inkling of what the French were doing and when he met Washington's troops at Yorktown he had no hesitation in putting the sea at his back. He thought of the sea as a friendly place occupied and controlled by his own side, and therefore an element of support and strength in land war. The greatest ally of the Americans was Cornwallis himself, who was as vain, incompetent and inflexible a man as appeared in either army during the Revolution. He marched boldly into the trap without pausing to investigate and without the slightest suspicion that it was a trap at all. An unsuspicious general is worth his weight in gold to the opposition. Cornwallis deserved the Congressional Medal of Honor. On October 19, 1781, he delivered himself and seven thousand men into the hands of the Colonials at Yorktown, and the look of baffled surprise on his face when he discovered that the ships in the bay were not British but French must surely have been one of the memorable moments of the whole war.

Yorktown is popularly thought of as the battle that brought the Revolutionary war to an end. But the war dragged on for another year and a half, and did not end until April 1783. Despite the surrender of Cornwallis, the British were still in possession of New York, Charleston, and other strategic areas. Skirmishes and maneuvers for territorial position continued. Though there were no more pitched combats, men were wounded and died, hopes for peace flared up and embered out. After Yorktown, De Grasse sailed off for the West Indies to protect the French islands, and was seen in America no more. Political crises continued through 1782 and Paine continued to produce his *Crisis* papers. Still, the feeling grew that the end of the war was not far off. Negotiations for an armistice began in Europe. Though these were delayed, though England continued to hope that the Colonies would still accept terms short of independence, though news traveled slowly and instructions took months to get back and forth across the Atlantic, events ground toward the conclusion made certain, if not immediate, by Yorktown.

It was a time of growing triumph for Paine as well as for the young nation about to be born. Free from financial worries, recognized as one of the great figures of the Revolution even by his enemies, held in warmest esteem by Franklin, Jefferson, and Washington himself, Paine's career in America was at its zenith. Never had his writing been so bold, confident, and powerful. The ideal of independence, toward which he had urged the Americans in 1775, was on the verge of realization, and the cymbals of success sounded loudly and sweetly in his ears. He strode through Philadelphia, supervised the publication of his pamphlets, carried on his extensive correspondence, was on the alert for signs of defeatism even at this late hour, with an energy and clarity of mind that were themselves indications of how well things were going.

Peace was proclaimed at last. British troops marched onto British vessels and sailed for home, while the Americans were released from service and went back to their farms. The long agony was over. Paine wrote the last ringing words of *Crisis XIII* even as Washington was summoned to the capital to be idolized by Congress. It was 1783. Paine was forty-six—in the prime of his life and at the high tide of personal and political success.

IRON BRIDGE

P EACE is a relief after war; it is also an anticlimax. After the tumult of the seven-year conflict, Paine found the sudden quiet deafening. He was profoundly happy that independence had been won, but he was also convinced that the important part of his career was over. Triumph and sadness, mixed together, made a strong brew, and he retired to private life with unsettled feelings tugging him in different directions.

There was a general exodus from Philadelphia after the

signing of the peace treaty. Congress moved to Princeton, New Jersey, and invited General Washington to make his headquarters there, that he might be appropriately honored. Washington settled in nearby Rocky Hill, where he was showered with gifts, praise, decorations, and even offers to be the first American king. He was plainly more suited by nature to be king than George III—who was soon to go mad and be confined in a strait-jacket for periodic intervals—but he saw no advantage to America in being ruled by a George I starting a new dynastic reign of a House of Washington. More firmly than Julius Caesar was reported to have done, Washington rejected the crown proffered to him more than once. But if there was such a thing as an American court, the victorious General was the center of it in the summer of 1783.

Paine, too, had left Philadelphia, and taken up lodgings not far away in a small house at Bordentown, New Jersey, next to his friend and comrade-in-arms Colonel Kirkbride. The two men, in addition to common political sentiments, shared a strong interest in science, and they set up a large shop-laboratory at home where they experimented away to their heart's content. America then, as now, had no great leaning toward pure science. Practical or applied science was all the rage, with Benjamin Franklin, that most practical of philosophers, leading the way. Paine was less concerned with discovering the secrets of Nature than with turning out improved models based on the latest scientific principles. He dabbled in tallow candles, paper money, steam engines, and dozens of other ingenious contraptions. Some of these he worked at in collaboration with Franklin, who had returned from his long diplomatic mission in France. But Paine's chief interest was an iron bridge.

In the eighteenth century bridges were for the most part made of wood, and were supported by a series of piers sunk into the river bed. Though cheap to construct, they wore out quickly. Rain and dampness rotted the wood of the superstructure and the constant water pressure undermined the piers and made them unsafe. They were designed by European engineers for use in European rivers. But European rivers were fairly narrow and slow-flowing. Compared with American rivers, the Seine, the Arno, the Tiber seemed not much larger than creeks, and even the Thames, the Rhine and the Danube were miniature next to the Hudson and the Mississippi. The wooden bridge with supporting piers, imported from Europe, did not stand up to the size and water volume of American rivers; it was not designed to do so. Here was an illogical situation crying for improvement, a challenge Paine could not resist.

He sought to escape the mortality of wood by building a bridge of iron. The second difficulty, the piers so vulnerable to water pressure, he leapfrogged altogether by designing a bridge with a single arch. It would have no piers in the river at all and would be held up by abutments on either shore. The design was at once simple and revolutionary. It would overcome the defects of the European bridge and create one more suited to American conditions. Paine approached this problem in engineering exactly as he did a problem in politics. What is wrong with the present situation, he asked first. What, in all logic, should be done, he asked next. He drew no distinction between *should* and *can*. The fact that bridges had never been made of iron and, for practical reasons, might not work bothered him not a whit. If it was logical that they should work, that was enough. The fact that colonies had not ever before rebelled successfully against their mother countries had not discouraged Paine, either. Under certain circumstances they should, and if they wanted to strongly enough, they would.

Precedent and past experience were factors to which Paine paid singularly little attention. In this sense he was very much a part of the American experience. America, after getting under way as an independent nation, prided itself on not being tied to the dead weight of the past, on not being slavishly bound by tradition. Living in the New World meant making a new start and breaking away from the old habits and customs of Europe. This feeling for life as an unformed adventure beginning now, was perfectly illustrated by Paine himself in the sphere both of ideas and scientific inventions. The iron bridge was created by the same man who wrote *Common Sense*.

At Bordentown, Paine made three small-scale models of his bridge; one in wood, one in cast iron, one in wrought iron. When they were finished, he loaded them on a cart and took them to Philadelphia, where for a time they were on display in the back yard of Franklin's house on Market Street. Crowds of visitors came to see them every day, exclaiming at their ingenuity, novelty, and miniature size.

Paine's original intention was to use his bridge to span the Schuylkill River, and to that end sought to interest the Pennsylvania Assembly in the project. Various members of the Assembly expressed their approval, but the idea was too daring for others. Engineers and bridge-builders were dubious about the sturdiness of the single arch, and felt that the added cost of the iron would not pay off in terms of added durability. Besides, they had grown up under the old English engineering manuals. It was hard for them to throw their early training overboard and start over again. The iron bridge aroused a considerable stir, but it led to nothing definite. Paine was advised to take his models to Europe. If he could get the support of the French Academy, and the endorsement of leading scientists in France and England, he would have a far better chance of floating his invention in America. The Colonies may have won their political independence from Great Britain, but in matters of culture and science, they were still wholly dependent on the Old World.

Before Paine could take his bridge to Europe, he had other urgent matters to settle. One of these was money, an old problem for him by now. With the end of the war the annual sum of eight hundred dollars he had been getting for writing in support of the Revolution also came to an end. He needed cash to live on and to pay for his experiments. He began writing letters to Congress describing his services to America and asking for recognition in some tangible form. At this time, Congress was handing out sums of money to various men in grateful recognition of their services during the Revolution. In terms of merit Paine felt himself to be the most deserving. Since he was a man who put a very high valuation on himself, his letters sang his own praises with unrestrained enthusiasm.

Paine's enemies in Congress were still active, and to their number were added those who disagreed with his stand for a strong central government. His pleas fell upon deaf ears. In despair he wrote to Washington complaining about the neglect and indifference shown him, and urging the General to plead his cause. Washington invited Paine to visit him at Rocky Hill, and appealed to Congress at once on Paine's behalf. For a time nothing happened. Paine accepted the General's invitation, and stayed at Rocky Hill as Washington's guest. While Congress was arguing his case, Paine commuted frequently to New York and resumed contact with his political and literary friends. Paine appreciated Washington's courtesy and hospitality, but like everyone else found the reserved Virginian a hard man to talk to.

In the following year, 1784, the country's debts to Paine were finally settled. New York awarded him a house and 277-acre farm at New Rochelle. This handsome property had been owned by a Loyalist family which abandoned it when the British withdrew. Paine went down to inspect the acreage, threw a party for the villagers to celebrate the occasion, then returned to Bordentown. Though Paine did not himself live on the farm until many years later, he rented it to tenant farmers, and the property yielded him a small steady income.

Meanwhile, the Virginia Assembly declined once and for all to bestow any honors upon him, a refusal balanced somewhat by the decision of the Pennsylvania Assembly to grant him an outright sum of five hundred pounds. And at last, after much debate and under relentless goading from Washington, to whom at this period it could refuse nothing, Congress grudgingly consented to give Paine three thousand dollars. It is doubtful whether this sum was enough to repay even his personal expenses on the vital mission to France in 1781. At any rate, he had to be content with it; he was to get no more.

The man who might have been rich, had he been willing to profit from the sale of his writings, was now to be poor because of the forgetfulness and partisanship of the government he had served. Governments have notoriously short memories. When crises are past, they quickly forget their fears and anxieties, and minimize the services of those on whose help they once desperately depended. Paine was, of course, foolish and naïve not to have known this. But even had he known it, it is doubtful that he would have acted otherwise. He approached money on the basis of principle rather than practicality, and was painfully hurt that everybody else approached it on the basis of practicality rather than principle. This was a discovery that he made over and over again, and he never adjusted himself to it. He continued to waste a good deal of time and energy scolding Congress, upbraiding powerful men who disagreed with his ideas, and badgering his friends for support—all because he refused to accept the way of the world.

Paine's entire approach to life was based on the widespread eighteenth-century belief that man was a reasonable animal. He was also convinced that man was essentially good, and once shown the sane, logical course of conduct, he would naturally embrace it. When men did not behave logically, reasonably or benevolently, Paine was outraged. They were not doing what they were supposed to do. He was always convinced, however, that this was a temporary condition, and that with further education the world would come round. This noble theory, resting on the belief that the goodness in human nature is stronger than the evil, animates the Declaration of Independence, and is the very theory which gave America its start in history. Paine insisted on applying it not simply to the general conduct of mankind but to every specific instance as well. He realized soon enough that in day-to-day affairs men often fell far short of the ideal. This condition he never accepted and never became reconciled to, with an unbending rigidity that caused him much personal grief.

What with his experiments and money troubles, the years passed and the trip to Europe kept getting postponed. Being the man he was, he could not keep altogether out of public disputes. The most savage one of the mid-1780's involved the uprisings of farmers against the banks to which they were heavily in debt. In 1786 the violent Shays' Rebellion, named after its militant leader, Daniel Shays, broke out in Massachusetts. This rebellion was so serious and, for a time, so widespread that it threatened to overthrow the government.

After the war, prices had risen steeply. Money drained out of the country in payment for needed imports from abroad. England, ordinarily one of America's richest markets, continued to boycott Colonial goods, which forced America to sell its surplus in other, less desirable markets at lower rates. This reduced the supply of currency still further. Farmers, who had borrowed money during the war to keep their farms going while they went off to fight, were unable to meet their mortgage payments. Many were dispossessed, and organized in angry groups which demanded that cheap paper money be printed so that their debts might be paid.

Any increase in the amount of paper money in circulation meant a lowering in the real value of the dollar. If you borrowed a hundred dollars from a bank when the dollar was high and repaid it when its value was low, obviously the bank would be the loser and you the gainer. The banks, naturally, clung to the hard money system; they saw themselves ruined by a flood of cheap and largely worthless paper money. In the Shays' Rebellion the farmers resisted by force the efforts of the banks to foreclose their land, and even demanded a flat cancellation of all their debts. Armed bands marched on the state capital. The uprising was suppressed by the militia only after a pitched battle near the arsenal in Springfield.

Paine's sympathies were largely with the farmers but his convictions were all on the side of the bankers. Flooding the country with paper money might temporarily solve the problems of the farmers but by creating an immense inflation it would ruin the economy. Besides, it could save the farmers only by destroying the merchants, and the prospect of setting class against class was hideous to

Paine. It did not square with his dream of a state in which the natural goodness of all men would shine through. The merchants and bankers had extended credit to the farmers in good faith; this credit represented their own honestly earned savings. If these debts were canceled, as cruel an injustice would be inflicted on the creditors as the debtors felt was being inflicted on themselves. If a man was carrying too heavy a burden, it was no help to the community if he transferred it to another man's back.

Paine wrote a pamphlet on paper money in which he defended the banks, chided the farmers, warned against sacrificing one class to satisfy another, and urged that terms of payment be eased—all in the general national interest. Needless to say, these ideas scarcely added to Paine's popularity with the mass of the population. During the war he had fought with the farmers and frontiersmen not only against the British but against those who would deprive them of the right to vote. Now he was against them, defending the very people he himself had attacked earlier. Some of the good will he had built up during the war began to melt away. It was hard for men, especially aroused and angry men, to put up with someone who defended the over-all interests of society against their own special needs. A farmer threatened with foreclosure was not likely to listen to someone urging him not to fight back, in the name of the greater good of society as a whole, even if that someone had successfully urged the farmer for seven years to fight the British, and urged so eloquently that there were people who said that the pen of Tom Paine was mightier than the sword of Washington.

Paine lived through this uproar much as he had through earlier ones. He was upset by the hostility of former friends. He was made angry by charges that he had deserted his own principles. But the thought of not sticking to his guns never for a moment occurred to him. He wasn't looking for votes or popularity. He was looking for truth. As always, if it came to a showdown between truth and friendship, he would let friendship go. This was Paine's great strength as a debater and pamphleteer. It was at the same time one of his great weaknesses as a human being. Unable to compromise or soften his ideas, he did not do well in the give-and-take of ordinary life. In a great crisis or emergency, his driving power was tremendously effective in arousing people from their usual habits. In normal times, this power was largely wasted; men went back to being themselves, caring much less about flaming principles and ideals than about getting along. In the long run, Paine's theories about debts, banks, and paper money were proven sound and became accepted practice in America. In the short run, they did his reputation far more harm than good.

Despite these occasional sallies into politics, Paine's life at this time was largely private. He was busy with the iron bridge, and the idea of returning to Europe was growing stronger in his mind. If he could win the approval of leading engineers in France and England, he might yet see his bridge spanning the Schuylkill River. At any rate he had exhausted present possibilities in America, and was assured by native contractors that approval of his invention by leading scientific groups abroad was the quickest way of breaking down resistance and reluctance at home. He had received a letter from his father, an old man now, urging him to return for a visit, and Tom was seized by a sudden longing to see his parents again before they died. His homing instinct, dormant these many years, flared up unexpectedly.

With no great public cause requiring his presence in America, Paine prepared for his European trip. He wrapped his few personal belongings with no great care, and then packed his bridge model very carefully indeed. Accompanied by Colonel Kirkbride, who was going to see him off, he rode from Bordentown to New York where, in April 1787, he sailed for France. He was fifty years old. He planned to remain in Europe for a few months, attend to the bridge, visit Thetford, come back to America, and settle down permanently in New Rochelle. If someone had told him as he embarked that he would remain in Europe for fifteen years, be caught up in another powerful revolutionary upheaval, spend ten months in prison, write two long and famous books, and not return to America until after the dawn of a new century, bruised in spirit and broken in health—he would have thought the man mad.

Paine's boat reached Brittany in May, and he coached to Paris along the valley of the Loire, then reaching its first spring bloom. Thomas Jefferson had succeeded Franklin as American minister to France. He and Paine had admired each other during the war years; they now became warm friends. Paine resumed the contacts with the French scientists and mathematicians which had begun six years before, when he had come to Paris in quest of a loan from the King. When his bridge model, delayed at customs, reached the capital, the French Academy of Sciences appointed a committee to examine it. After due deliberation, this body gave its approval to the principle of the new bridge, and Paine, greatly encouraged, sent it on to Sir Joseph Banks, the president of the Royal Society in London.

He himself reached London in August 1787, and, after making sure that the bridge model was being surveyed by the scientists of the Royal Society, left almost at once for Thetford. He got there too late to see his father, who had died in the summer, but his mother, at ninety, was still in good health. She had said harsh things of Tom before, but she now repented having ever accused him of being an "undutiful son." Some months before, he had settled a weekly pension of nine shillings

upon her for life, allowing her to live in reasonable comfort until her death, which came four years later. In the
fifteen years since he had last been there, Thetford
seemed not to have changed at all. The school, the wind-
ing, cobbled main street, the Quaker meeting house, the
crumbling walls of an abandoned Catholic abbey, the
guildhall where the local politicians still sold political
offices to the highest bidders, the flat Norfolk countryside—these were as before. The cities of England were
being transformed by the first factories of the Industrial
Revolution. By contrast, the villages appeared not only
unchanged, but somehow more themselves than ever.

French approval of the bridge was now followed by
British. When the favorable pronouncement was issued
by the Royal Academy, manufacturers in England became interested. The firm of Walker in Rotherham,
Yorkshire, made Paine an offer to build, which he accepted. Since his presence was needed at the construction
works, he put off his return to America for a year and
prepared to spend as much of 1788 as was needed to get
his bridge well launched. He commuted between London and Yorkshire, took an active part in the details of
construction, and worked out a plan with the Messrs.
Walker for sharing the expenses and profits of the bridge
after it was built. The plan was to exhibit the bridge in
London, stimulate interest in its sale, and thus attract a
maximum price. In due time the plan was carried out.

The finished bridge was shipped by water from York-shire and put on exhibition on Paddington Green, London, where thousands of persons paid a shilling apiece to see it. Paine seemed well on his way to fortune.

Fortune, however, was not destined to be his lot in life. Before his business venture could be brought to its conclusion, the French Revolution burst upon the world. On July 14, 1789, the Bastille was stormed, casting all Europe into a turbulent fury which was to last for twenty-five years. The upheaval in France drew Paine irresistibly. He put aside his bridge and plunged headlong into the new torrent.

THE RIGHTS OF MAN

THE French Revolution came as a great surprise to Paine, as to nearly everyone else. When he arrived in France in 1787, conditions seemed no worse than during his previous visit in 1781. The life of the huge numbers of poor was wretched, Paris was crowded with beggars, the French reformers and philosophers were satirizing and protesting the incompetence of the Bourbon regime, the middle class was clamoring for privilege and power—but not apparently more so than ever. Then, suddenly, on July 14, 1789, came the storming of the Bastille and the release of its prisoners. The whole of Europe was startled and shaken.

Shuttling back and forth between France and England during 1787–1789, Paine had no inkling that things were about to pop. Yet he was by this time an experienced observer, a veteran revolutionary, and an ardent believer that the American example was bound to spread to Europe. He had easy entree to the counsels of influential men, though he continued to spend a good deal of his time in taverns and public houses in contact with plain people. Rubbing shoulders with high and low, he was in an ideal position to predict what would happen. But living through great events is not always a guarantee that one sees them coming. Paine may have been overjoyed by the rising of the Parisians, but like the rest of Europe he was also amazed.

Though, to be sure, he was absorbed in the affairs of the iron bridge, he had time for politics too. On reaching England late in 1787, he was greeted with great hospitality and enthusiasm by Edmund Burke and other leading Whigs. Burke was the famous parliamentary orator whose speech *On Conciliation with America* had argued the cause of the Colonies in 1775 with unsurpassed fervor and eloquence. Burke's advice to his own government to be generous had gone unheeded, and America was lost to the British Empire. The Whigs were about to return to power and anxious to restore trade with the

New World. Paine was looked upon as a leading American of great influence and reputation. To court him and win his favor seemed a quick way of speeding up good relations with America and bringing business back to normal.

Paine was therefore given the "English weekend" treatment. He was introduced to the Duke of Portland, the Marquis of Lansdowne, Charles James Fox, and other leading Whigs. He spent long weekends at their country estates and at Burke's, sat at dinner with earls and duchesses, was praised, flattered, attended to—not for his beautiful blue eyes or his handsome presence or even his ideas, but because of the power of his pen and his possible usefulness as a Whig instrument in cementing relations with the United States. Paine enjoyed all this attention. He would not have been human if he had not. As he moved in these luxurious and aristocratic surroundings, he thought of his earlier years in England when, obscure and unnoticed, he had been barely able to survive. What a queer thing fortune was, and how it blew men up and down.

Paine was not the man to be won over in this way. He had his share of vanity, but it was the vanity of ideas and not the vanity of pride. He ate and drank heartily, held up his end of the conversation, took part in everything that was going on. But when his hosts spoke of trade, he spoke of democracy. When they talked of the growing liberalism of British foreign policy, he brought up the rotten boroughs in Parliament, the slums of the poor, the grinding anguish of women and children huddled at the bottom of the social ladder. They spoke of reform, he of revolution. They urged the need to move forward but to move slowly, he argued the necessity of haste. They referred to politics as a game, he as a passion.

Nor was it his ideas alone that proved stubborn and unyielding. So were his manners and dress. He ate heartily enough but not daintily, and without that grace and delicacy of movement favored by the fops, dandies, and titled gentlemen of the time. As for his clothes and appearance, they too remained unaltered. He wore the same coarse homespun as before. His wig was unpowdered and never on quite straight. His breeches needed pressing and his black hose were never pulled up tight enough. The large silver buckles on his shoes were the only elegance he allowed himself. He was, in short, a rough-looking customer, and he must have cut a startling figure in the rich salons of a period in English life when elegant grooming was very much the order of the day.

When the Whig wooing of Paine produced no visible results, it began to cool off, and Paine was slowly eased out of their picture. He began hearing less often from his friend Burke, and invitations to dine at the Duke of Portland's became infrequent. When the French Revolution erupted, his love affair with the Whigs broke off altogether. The storming of the Bastille and the events that followed split the Whig party down the middle. The liberal wing, led by Fox, sympathized with the French uprising and regarded it as a movement to reform the monarchy and make it constitutional on the English model. The conservative wing, of which Burke was the spearhead, was dismayed by the events in France and thus moved closer to the Tories, who damned the French Revolution and all its ways. The Whigs did come to power but their reign was short-lived. Harassed by their own internal divisions, they could not command a majority in Parliament. They were soon succeeded by the Tories who, chiefly under the leadership of their great prime minister, the younger Pitt, were to remain in unbroken power for more than twenty years. Their policy during this whole time was simple: all-out hostility to the social upheaval in France.

Burke's feelings about the French Revolution were summarized in his famous tract, *Reflections on the Revolution in France*, which appeared late in 1790. Some months before its appearance, Paine had been in Paris, where Lafayette gave him the key to the Bastille and asked that he send it to George Washington with the compliments of the French nation. This Paine did, and the huge iron key hangs on a wall in Mount Vernon to this day. Accompanying the key was a letter in which Paine set forth the prospects for French reform and compared them favorably with the American revolution. Late in 1789 and early in 1790 such comparisons were still possible. The early aims of the French Revolution seemed fairly moderate. Its leaders wanted to curb the Bourbons, not overthrow them. They strove for a democratic National Assembly and better living conditions, and deplored unnecessary violence and mob action. Paine was in sympathy with most of these ideas. When Burke's attack on the French Revolution came out, Paine's mind was already made up. He sat down at once in his London inn to compose a reply. The reply, written at Paine's usual breakneck pace, appeared early in 1791. It was called *The Rights of Man*.

Burke had two reasons for regarding the French Revolution with alarm. The first was its attack on law and order. Since the monarchy had been accepted by the French for many centuries, it was a legitimate government and could not be overthrown from one moment to the next. Any attempt to do so would undermine government altogether and substitute mob rule where any group, strong and violent enough, might set itself up in power. Governments that had been sanctified by tradition might be reformed or even overhauled; but overthrown they could not be without endangering the fabric of society itself. In England, Burke claimed, there had been a similar situation a century earlier. The bloodless revolution of 1688 had established the supremacy of the House of Commons over a constitutional monarch. This happy arrangement was not to be overthrown every time some group in the population was dissatisfied with it. The principle of established order, hallowed by general acceptance, was infinitely preferable to the principle of anarchy and chaos when greed, passion, and ruthlessness were given free reign. Better, said Burke, an established and legitimate government full of injustice than an unsettled government violently arrived at in justice's name.

His second reason was practical rather than theoretical. He feared the excesses of the Revolution. The assault on the Bastille had shocked him deeply, and the thought of mob rule made him shudder. If even this much were allowed to happen, nothing and no one was safe, and any horror was possible. Three years before the Reign of Terror, Burke was already warning against it as the logical result of the storming of the Bastille. In a series of remarkable prophecies he foresaw the execution of King and Queen, the Terror, the slaughter of the aristocracy, and the appearance of a military dictator. The whole course of the Revolution on its destructive side, from the beheading of Louis XVI and Marie Antoinette to the rise of Napoleon, was charted by Burke and served as the climax of his *Reflections*. The book sold for three shillings—a high price. Thousands of copies were bought up and distributed in royal and noble circles throughout

Europe. George III praised it, the first kind words he had ever uttered about Burke.

In *The Rights of Man* Paine attacked Burke's reliance on the past. He repudiated the claim that the Constitution of 1688 was law in England for all time:

> There never did, nor never can exist a parliament . . . possessed of the right of binding . . . posterity to the "end of time." . . . Every age and generation must be free to act for itself, *in all cases.* . . . Man has no property in man. . . . The parliament or the people of 1688, or of any other period, had no more right to dispose of the people of the present . . . than the parliament or the people of the present day have to . . . control those who are to live an hundred or a thousand years hence . . . It is the living and not the dead, that are to be accommodated.

Paine then summed up relations between past and present in one of his powerful sentences:

> If the present generation, or any other, are disposed to be slaves, it does not lessen the rights of the succeeding generation to be free: wrongs cannot have legal descent.

A basic right of man was the right to be judged on his own merits and not on the accident of birth. Paine let loose a heavy barrage against one of his pet peeves—the titled aristocracy. After blasting away at earls, dukes and kings in general, he got around to France in particular: "It is, properly, from . . . France that the folly of titles has been abolished. It has out-grown the baby-clothes of count and duke, and breeched itself in manhood." This section of *The Rights of Man*, more than any other, outraged the authorities in England and caused them to look on Paine as a dangerous man, concerned not only with Colonial independence but with undermining the British system itself.

As for Burke's second argument, the excesses of the Revolution, Paine had some sharp comments on this, too. If brutalities were committed by the people, he said, it was the fault of the Bourbon regime under which they had lived and by which they had been oppressed for centuries. Their masters had taught them no better, another reason for throwing out rulers who had not improved the character of their subjects. And why, asked Paine, did Burke shed so many tears over the possible fate of Marie Antoinette but had none to spare for the millions of wretched Frenchmen suffering under her rule and her husband's? So one-sided a sympathy cast doubt on the fairness of Burke's observations. Moreover, his prophecies on the course the Revolution would take, Paine continued, were so much guesswork, and one man's guess was as good as another's. (In these prophecies, Burke was proven right, Paine wrong.) But even should they all come to pass, Paine concluded, the French were justified in revolting against oppression.

In his earlier association with Burke, Paine had learned of the annual pension of fifteen hundred pounds which the Irish orator had for some years been secretly receiving from the Crown, and of his ambition (soon to be realized) to have this pension increased. He therefore looked upon Burke's *Reflections* as dishonest from the start, as corrupted by self-interest and the desire for personal gain, and as a crude attempt to win the favor of the British King. To Paine's usual confident tone was added a note of righteousness that made *The Rights of Man* sound a bit like the Ten Commandments. Paine was never more sure of himself, of the soundness of his ideas, of the world being his oyster, and of the French Revolution as the second installment of his conviction that all countries would soon be republican. He wound up his reply to Burke with a ringing statement on knowledge and ignorance:

> The revolutions of America and France have thrown a beam of light over the world, which reaches into man. . . . Ignorance is of a peculiar nature: once dispelled, it is impossible to reestablish it. It is not originally a thing of itself, but is only the absence of knowledge; and though man may be *kept* ignorant, he cannot be *made* ignorant. The mind, in discovering truths, acts in the same manner as it acts through the eye in discovering an object; when once any object has been seen, it is impossible to put the mind back to the same condition it was in before it

saw it. Those who talk of a counter-revolution in France, show how little they understand of man. . . . The means must be an obliteration of knowledge; and it has never yet been discovered how to make a man unknow his knowledge, or unthink his thoughts.

Paine never doubted for a moment that he had utterly demolished Burke and that, on paper at least, nothing more remained to be said on the subject.

His sense of optimism about the future of man was reinforced by Paine's personal happiness and sense of well-being at this time. *The Rights of Man*, despite its high three-shilling price, was selling like hotcakes and soon outstripped Burke's pamphlet, which had been offered to the public at the same price. The iron bridge, on exhibition at Paddington, had not yet found a buyer, but the public was thronging to see it in great numbers. In London Paine was lodging with Thomas Rickman and his family, all of whom had become his close friends. Rickman was a bookseller and musician of strong republican sympathies, who named his children after leading revolutionaries of the day. His eldest son, Thomas Paine Rickman, had been thus christened after the success of the *Crisis* papers.

At the Rickmans', Paine was not only the star boarder but the center of a new group of friends. These included Priestley, the chemist; Romney, the painter, whose portrait of Paine is perhaps the most famous likeness; William Blake, the great mystical poet and engraver; Godwin, the radical thinker whose book *Political Justice* (1796) was to have a profound effect on a whole generation of English youth; and Lord Edward Fitzgerald, an Irish firebrand, later to figure in one of the periodic Irish outbreaks against the English occupation. These were men whose reputations were still to be made, a significant change from the established Whigs of the Burke circle who had embraced Paine when he first arrived. Drawn together by a common desire to reform British political life, they became good friends as well. They met not only at the Rickmans' but at the White Bear Tavern in Piccadilly. They sang and played chess and dominoes when they were not engaged in lively discussion.

In the summer of 1791 Paine was back in Paris, arranging for the French translation of *The Rights of Man*. The quiet phase of the Revolution was approaching its end. After the fall of the Bastille, Louis XVI had been petitioned to summon an Estates-General or Constitutional Assembly to reform and liberalize the Constitution. This Louis had agreed to do, and in other ways appeared to have accepted the Revolution. His willingness to give way had strengthened the hand of the moderates, led by Lafayette and Mirabeau, and the country appeared to be moving in the direction of a constitutional monarchy much in the English fashion. But the King was secretly in touch with court circles and monarchs of other countries, and one afternoon, disguised as a valet, he slipped with his family out of the Louvre Palace and made for the border.

At the village of Varennes, near the Belgian frontier, he was detected by an innkeeper suspicious of a fifty-*livre* piece Louis asked him to change. The royal family was thereupon bundled back to Paris. When news of the attempted escape became public, crowds lined the streets of every town to hiss and boo the carriage bringing Louis XVI and Marie Antoinette in humiliation back to their capital. The crowds were aroused by a sense of having been abandoned and betrayed by their rulers, and were egged on by the more extremist orators who had argued all along that Louis was secretly conspiring with the foreign enemies of France. In Paris, Paine found himself in a huge crowd of angry Frenchmen waiting for the return of their monarch. They were all wearing revolutionary cockades in their hats. All but Paine. Suspecting him of being a royalist, the crowd set upon him with angry cries. Since Paine could not speak French, he was unable to explain matters to his assailants and, but for the last-minute intervention of an English-speaking Parisian, might have been hanged on the spot.

This narrow escape did not dampen his enthusiasm. He proceeded to form a Republican Society with four other members, Condorcet, Brissot, Duchâtelet and Bonneville. At a time when Danton, Robespierre, and the extreme radicals were still thinking of a limited monarchy, Paine's Society issued proclamations calling for a republic, referred to Louis XVI as Louis Capet, and urged France not to waste any further emotion over the individual persons of the King and Queen. On this occasion Paine was too far ahead of history. Royalist sentiment had not yet run its course, and the French were not yet ready to attack the persons of King and Queen. Paine and his group argued freely and energetically in a Paris full of other clubs and groups also arguing freely and issuing countless manifestoes. French society was in a ferment; for the first time in centuries, almost anyone could say and write what he pleased, a situation made to order for Paine and very akin to America in 1775. Paine enjoyed this period immensely.

Late in 1791 he returned to England, where the popularity and mass sale of *The Rights of Man* were seriously disturbing the Tory government, now under the leadership of the younger Pitt. Pitt was a clever man, devoted to the policy of doing nothing about troublemakers unless absolutely necessary. He knew the immense publicity value attached to persecution and martyrdom, and realized that nothing could kill a movement or idea faster than ignoring it. He decided, therefore, to ignore Paine. When *The Rights of Man* appeared in a three-shilling edition, he hoped it would prove too expensive for mass circulation. But despite the price, the book sold widely and the government had to take steps to undo the damage. As its first move, the government commissioned an officeholder named George Chalmers to write a mud-slinging biography of Paine. Chalmers published his book under the pen name Francis Oldys; it did much to circulate the old rumors of Paine's drunkenness and unreliability.

The Rights of Man was dedicated to George Washington. Paine sent fifty copies to his old friend, now the first President of the United States, together with several to Thomas Jefferson, the Secretary of State. Washington was displeased by the book. He was trying to re-establish good relations with England. Anything from an American source that offended the English government seemed to Washington unfortunate. Besides, now that the war for independence was won, the General's naturally conservative instincts came to the fore again. He himself did not wish to be a king, but he had no distaste for kings as such, and Paine's violent anti-royalist sentiments left him cold. He was therefore annoyed at the dedication; no man likes to be associated with a book whose point of view he does not share. After a long delay, he sent Paine a note which made no direct reference to *The Rights of Man* but expressed vague good wishes for the author's future prospects.

But if the book irritated the President, it filled his

Secretary of State with great enthusiasm. Jefferson was having serious differences of opinion with John Adams, the Vice President, and Alexander Hamilton, the Secretary of the Treasury. Of all the men around Washington, Adams was the most sympathetic to royalty, while Hamilton, convinced that the mass of people were an irresponsible mob incapable of ruling themselves, was striving to set up high property qualifications for voters. Jefferson, by contrast, was strongly committed to republicanism, and wished to extend political power to the whole population. Only the harmonizing genius of Washington kept these warring personalities and conflicting opinions working together in the same cabinet.

Even Washington's tactful authority was strained to the breaking point when Jefferson sent *The Rights of Man* to its American printer with an accompanying letter expressing the feeling that it would discredit "the *political heresies* which have sprung up among us" and that "our citizens will *rally* a second time around the standard of *Common Sense*." The letter was printed without Jefferson's consent, arousing a storm in the press for and against Adams. Adams protested his innocence of royalist convictions and asked Jefferson to repudiate his statement about "political heresies." Washington intervened, ruffled feelings were smoothed down, the matter settled for the time being. Jefferson, himself an able politician, recognized that the time was not yet ripe for

his more advanced ideas, and made his peace with Adams.
But when he and his close associate James Madison urged
Washington to make Paine a cabinet member, the Presi-
dent firmly refused, and the popular success of *The
Rights of Man* in America did nothing to change his
mind.

Paine had earned more than a thousand pounds from
the English sale alone, and, characteristically, he turned
most of this money over to the Society for Constitutional
Reform. Burke, meanwhile, had come forth with a new
pamphlet *Appeal from the New to the Old Whigs*, in
which he carried the ideas introduced in *Reflections* to
their logical extreme. He quoted extensively from *The
Rights of Man* without, however, mentioning it by name.
There was little attempt to refute by analysis Paine's
arguments; Burke simply branded them insolent and
proposed "criminal justice" for men who believed in
them. He reaffirmed that England was committed to the
precedents and traditions of the past, and that the French
Revolution was run by bloodthirsty ruffians. No man
and no argument could have goaded Paine into a quicker
reply. He sat down to prepare what was to be Part II
of *The Rights of Man*.

When Pitt got wind of this new project, he set out
to forestall Paine. He engaged a publisher named Chapman to offer Paine a large sum for the rights to Part II.
Paine accepted at first, but when Chapman insisted on

the right to edit the text, author and publisher quarreled and the deal fell through. Paine went to other publishers. Despite the prospects of a profitable sale, they were reluctant to accept the piece. Word had been circulated that the government disapproved of Paine and might deal harshly with a printer who did business with him. After much searching, he found an obscure printer named Jordan who agreed to publish the pamphlet, but only after Paine had signed a statement assuming full legal responsibility for its contents. After various delays Part II came out in February 1792.

Where Part I dealt with a specific defense of the French, Part II drew up a detailed indictment of the English. Paine observed that the Bill of Rights promised by the Revolution of 1688 was largely a piece of paper to the mass of the population. Any mechanic in the kingdom could do a better and less expensive job of ruling England than his "Mad-jesty" King George III. The money the English government spent on wars would provide old-age pensions for everybody in the country over fifty. Paine analyzed the budget in detail, identified the huge number of useless jobs filled by friends and relatives of the party in power, and summed up the waste of public money. All governments are bad, he observed, but that founded on the principle of royalty and aristocracy is the worst.

All this was peculiarly painful to the British government. Here was a man who had cost the Empire its American Colonies, and now had the insolence to set up headquarters in London itself where he was thrusting a sharp sword into the vitals of the English system at home. Pitt conceded in private that Paine was right in many of his charges, but if his words were taken to heart a revolution was unavoidable. And Paine's standards of justice involved eliminating poverty, emptying the dungeons of prisoners and the jails of beggars, providing for the aged, doing away with oppressive taxes, and a host of other reforms beyond the power of any government to achieve without a complete overhauling of the social and political structure. It was exactly such an overhauling that Paine was crying for. The fact that it had already been achieved in America was what gave men their beginning hope.

> So deeply rooted were all the governments of the old world, [wrote Paine] and so effectually had . . . tyranny . . . established itself over the mind, that no beginning could be made in Asia, Africa or Europe, to reform the political condition of man. Freedom had been hunted round the globe; reason was considered as rebellion, and the slavery of fear had made men afraid to think.
>
> But such is the irresistible nature of truth, that all it asks, and all it wants, is the liberty of appearing. The sun needs no inscription to distinguish him from darkness, and no sooner did the American govern-

ments display themselves to the world, than despotism felt a shock, and men began to contemplate redress.

The examples of America and France now gave England her chance:

> Never did so great an opportunity offer itself to England, and to all Europe, as is produced by the two revolutions of America and France. By the former, freedom has a national champion in the western world; and by the latter, in Europe. . . . To use a trite expression, the iron is becoming hot. . . . The insulted German and the enslaved Spaniard, the Russ and the Pole are beginning to think. The present age will hereafter . . . be called The Age of Reason, and the present generation will appear to the future, as the Adam of a new world.

Part II is dedicated to Lafayette, to whom Paine offers his services in whatsoever capacity the Frenchman sees fit. The pamphlet breathes a fiery self-confidence which at times spills over into boastful conceit. In one of his rare autobiographical moments, Paine writes of himself:

> I have not only contributed to raise a new empire in the world, founded on a new system of government, but I have arrived at an eminence in political literature, the most difficult of all lines to succeed and excel in, which aristocracy, with all its aids, has not been able to reach or rival.

The last man in England to dispute Paine's boast of his eminence in political literature was Pitt. He hoped once more that Part II would not sell well. It was, in fact, a less interesting piece of writing than Part I, large sections of it being concerned with technical matters like the budget. Yet in the three months after publication some forty-five thousand copies were sold. By May of 1792, its success was assured. Pitt could afford to wait no longer.

His first act was a move against the printer. Jordan was arrested and the printing plates used for Part II confiscated. The police raided bookstalls all over England, seizing copies of the pamphlet. Gangs of bullies were hired to rouse mobs to bonfires where *The Rights of Man* was burned with violent public ceremony. The words *Tom Paine* were painted on shoe soles and the initials *TP* lettered on nail heads so that they might be stepped on daily. Charges of sedition were filed against Paine himself, and the date of his trial on the charge of seeking to overthrow the state set for the fall. The government paid hack writers from Grub Street to compose scandalous verses about Paine, raking up all the old rumors about him and ridiculing him mercilessly. His wax image was hanged in effigy on many a village green, and his name in the year 1792 became one of the most hated in England. The power of the government in terms of money, influence with the press, and ability to mold public opinion was immense, and most of it was turned full force on the task of discrediting Paine and all his works.

A campaign of this kind from so powerful an enemy would have been enough to intimidate most men. It only stimulated and encouraged Paine. He thrived on opposition and felt that ideas did, too. If they couldn't make their way in the open marketplace of competition, they weren't worth supporting. Besides, the minute Pitt's heavy guns went into action, Paine knew he had become dangerous to the whole system of royalist rule, and that his doctrines were making deep inroads in the minds of the English. He therefore welcomed official persecution as proof of his own success.

His friends kept urging him to be cautious, to lie low, but he only laughed and carried on more actively than ever. Throughout the summer he argued in taverns, spoke at outdoor rallies of republican societies, wrote short pieces for whatever papers or magazines could be induced to print them, and defied the authorities. He looked forward to his trial for sedition as an arena where he would once again present and dramatize his ideas before the world. All in all, he was never so animated and energetic, so filled with a sense of his own importance, so eager to do battle even with the great Tory dragon itself whose brain was the redoubtable Pitt.

The one final step the Prime Minister still hesitated to

take was to arrest Paine and keep him in jail until the trial. He was afraid of turning him into a martyr. Other reformers with large followings had been imprisoned; the result was a wave of public sympathy and an added frenzy of enthusiasm among their supporters. Much better to destroy their works, isolate them from publishers, blacken their names, make it dangerous to associate with them, even bring them up for trial. But jailing them was a last resort at best, to be avoided if possible. Paine was bothered; he was harried; he was tormented; but he was not arrested.

His friends, however, were always afraid that he would be, and begged him to leave the country. Rickman was convinced that a government agent was shadowing Paine, and keeping close tabs not only on his movements but on everybody who visited Rickman's house. Priestley's home was burned by a mob incited by hirelings. At Jordan's trial, the publisher refused Paine's offer to defend him, pleaded guilty, was let off with a suspended sentence, and told by the court to go home and sin no more. Wax effigies of Paine, with needles stuck in them, began appearing in public squares; and on Guy Fawkes Day, Paine began replacing Guy Fawkes as the national villain in some English towns. Edicts were issued banning the sale of his earlier books, but this only increased the demand for them and resulted in a huge under-the-counter sale. At mass meetings organized in town halls, at the private clubs, salons and chocolate houses frequented by the nobility, both Tory and Whig, Paine was denounced as a traitor and seditionist in language as violent as he himself had used against the King. Voices were raised in Parliament demanding his arrest and execution. He became a symbol of hope and of hatred, of reform and of connivance with the threat from France, a friend of the outraged masses and a dangerous termite seeking to destroy the established order. And the government still held off, still refrained from pouncing on him and clapping him behind bars.

The growing persecution of the republicans soon lopped off the less stouthearted members, and by the end of the summer Paine and his open sympathizers were down to a hard core. He had, of course, uncounted friends and partisans in the population as a whole, but the articulate ones among them felt it more prudent to remain silent and nurse their passions in private. Paine's own response to pressure was exactly the opposite. The more he was hanged in effigy, the more frequently he himself appeared in public. The more loudly he was denounced in the fashionable eating places, the more he harangued the customers at the White Bear. As the official campaign to keep him quiet grew, the noisier he became.

With fear of France growing in England, he chose to defend the French in all their new ways. As the English sought to forget the painful memory of their American defeat, Paine kept poking at this old wound by constantly taunting the King for his stupidity at the loss of the rich Colonies. With police agents buzzing around on all sides, taking careful notes on everything he said, his words grew even bolder (if that were possible), his attacks on the government gained heat and fury, his intoxication with his dream of the future grew more feverish than ever. For a time it seemed that in 1792 the whole of English political life was centered on Tom Paine, and his name was more frequently pronounced than that of any other man in the country. The Thetford staymaker had come a long way. The obscurity from which he had suffered as a young man in his twenties was now more than made up for by the fame and notoriety of the middle-aged man in his fifties.

In France a new National Convention was being elected, and no fewer than three districts selected Paine as their delegate. These were honors that he could scarcely refuse, and he began making plans for a return to France. Of the three districts, the town of Calais had elected him first, and it was this appointment that he decided to accept. He sent courtly letters to all three areas expressing his gratitude in elevated terms.

His trial for sedition was now rapidly approaching. He was looking forward to it eagerly, certain of his acquittal, confident that he would then journey to France in vindicated triumph. The public temper began rising in ugliness against Paine; the note of violence in the speeches against him grew harsher. His friends, increasingly alarmed, renewed their pleas that he get out of the country while the getting was good. He had made his points, they argued; he had said everything he had to say; his services were more needed in France than in England. Besides, Pitt might change his mind at any moment and decide to arrest him. Of what use would he be to anyone in jail?

Paine had no desire to be a martyr, even had he been convinced that martyrdom would have publicized his ideas. But he did not wish to run away from a fight, either, and the forthcoming trial was a challenge he found hard to pass up. By July and August, however, even he had to admit that the pressure was growing more serious. He was still not ready to admit that discretion was the better part of valor, but when Rickman began warning him that his continued presence in England was endangering his friends and exposing their families to official persecution, he began giving thought to flight.

Besides, argued his friends, events in France were marching forward at great speed; the lines between royalists and republicans were being drawn ever more sharply; armies from Austria and Germany, supported by England, were massing on the borders of France, threatening the Revolution. The pull of history was drawing Paine to France. Even he could see that though his pamphlets and ideas were making headway in England, change was a long way off. The Tory government, under its determined and able Prime Minister, was growing in power every day. Though reluctant to leave England, he might after all do more good in France. At least for the present. So reasoned Paine's friends, and urged him to fly.

Still he hesitated, still he continued his republican speechmaking. One day early in September, after an open-air meeting on behalf of the Society for Constitutional Reform, Paine was approached by William Blake. The poet was extremely agitated, and warned Paine not to return to his lodgings at Rickman's, for the police were there waiting to arrest him. He himself had just come from there with a portmanteau containing Paine's papers and some articles of clothing. Blake begged his friend to flee the country at once, in tones so eloquent that on the spur of the moment Paine agreed. They went to the nearest livery stable, where Paine hired a horse. He bade Blake farewell and set off on the road for Dover.

When the police discovered that Paine was apparently not returning, they suspected what was taking place, traced his movements, and dispatched two armed constables with the warrant for his arrest. These men took the Dover road not an hour behind Paine. Paine changed horses at Rochester and again at Canterbury; four hours after leaving London he reached Dover. As it happened, the packet for Calais was preparing to sail as he arrived. The customs guards had no reason to be suspicious; still, they made their way slowly through his belongings. But when they came upon a letter to Paine from George Washington, they looked up with sudden respect. Washington was a legendary name in England. His signature on a letter was enough to win for the bearer the treatment reserved for important personages. The guards ended their inspection, saluted Paine as they handed him his portmanteau, and waved him onto the boat. The vessel cast off and headed into the Channel. It had barely gotten under way when the two King's constables on steaming horses raced onto the pier, waving papers above their heads. But they were too late. Paine was already out of reach.

Thus did Paine leave his native country, one jump ahead of the police, their hot breath upon him in an escape delayed to the last breathtaking moment. But hunted or not, as the white chalk of the Dover cliffs faded in the Channel mist, Paine, being the man he was, must have been certain that he would one day return.

In this he was at once right and wrong. His bones were to be buried in English soil. But he was not again to see England alive.

THE
REIGN OF TERROR

W HEN the news of Paine's sudden arrival from England spread through Calais, hundreds of cheering
Frenchmen crowded into the dock area and greeted him
with deafening enthusiasm. When they learned about the
warrant for his arrest, Paine's new constituents received
their representative to the National Convention as a hero
returning from the jaws of death. The fact that he could
not address them in their own language did not dampen
their excitement. His remarks, translated on the spot,
sounded as meaningful to them as though they had been
delivered in French. He was given the full treatment—

speeches at the pier, a parade through the streets with hundreds of voices shouting *"Vive* Thomas Paine," and a triumphant appearance at the theater that evening.

Five days later he was in Paris, after a leisurely trip punctuated by celebrations in several towns en route. When he made his first appearance before the Convention, the entire hall rose to a man and cheered him noisily for several minutes. The new revolutionary calendar had just been put in force. It was now the Year One, a date that coincided neatly with Paine's debut as a French legislator.

Two weeks before, the Convention had passed a decree ousting the monarchy and declaring the country a republic. This seemed to Paine the happiest of omens. The week before, a French army under General Dumouriez had scored a crushing victory at Valmy over an invasion force under the Duke of Brunswick, coming to free the French King and put down the Revolution. Paris was seething with excitement.

The Convention—indeed the Revolution—was divided between two parties: the Girondins and the Jacobins, sometimes referred to as the Plain and the Mountain, since the one was seated on the main floor and the other in the balcony. The Girondins were the more moderate. They wanted reforms but in a slow, orderly way. They represented the middle class, by and large, and their policies were marked by the middle-class distaste for violence. The Jacobins were more radical and allied themselves with the propertyless masses. When things did not suit them, they roused the Parisian mob, which would then pack the Convention hall or the streets and boo the other side. It was the Jacobins who were to organize the Reign of Terror, and, as so often happens in revolutions, were themselves to be destroyed by it.

Paine was drawn naturally to the Girondins, whose leaders, Lafayette, Mirabeau, Brissot, and for a while Danton (before he switched to the Jacobins and was guillotined anyway when his policies proved too restrained), were his personal friends. He was in favor of violence if violence was necessary, but needless violence appalled him, and the ruthless Jacobin propaganda among the brutalized elements of the Parisian population seemed to him a dangerous political weapon. It appealed to the passions of man and not to his reason, and the road to the new world, Paine was convinced, lay only through reason. He listened to the speeches of the Jacobin leaders with growing alarm. It was hard to say which of them alarmed him most: the aggressive, tub-thumping Marat, the excitable orator Robespierre, who could sometimes sound sweetly reasonable, or the cold Saint-Just.

The great issue being debated when Paine assumed his seat was what to do with the person of the deposed King. The Jacobins wanted to execute him, the Girondins to let him be. Papers were discovered which revealed that

Louis was in secret correspondence with the rulers of other countries then at war with France, and this was used to whip up public feeling against him. Paine's approach to the question was characteristically simple. Louis XVI was now plain Louis Capet, he observed, and a menace to no one. If his presence in France kept alive the hopes of the displaced royalists, banish him for life. But do not kill him. His death, aside from its needlessness, would only arouse France's enemies to new fury. Besides, Paine pleaded, Louis had come to the aid of the American Revolution at critical times, and if he were beheaded, the reaction in America would be very bad.

These ideas were embodied in a speech delivered before the Convention in January 1793. Since Paine could not speak French, the speech was read by another deputy with Paine standing by his side. When the plea for sparing the King's life was made, Marat rose to his feet and shouted that Paine was against capital punishment because he was a Quaker, which disqualified him from discussing the subject. Paine denied this, and referred to his attack on the Quakers of Philadelphia as proof that he was not bound by Quaker principles. The speech went on. A few passages later, it was again interrupted by Marat, who argued that these could not be the sentiments of Thomas Paine, world-famous revolutionary, that they had been changed in translation by the Girondins. By the time these remarks were translated to Paine and he announced that the sentiments of the address were truly his, momentum had been lost, and the speech, when resumed with further interruptions still to come, never regained the drive and steam with which it had begun. Paine, standing by the rostrum, unable to follow quickly the exchanges in French between the warring parties in the Chamber, cut a curiously dignified and isolated figure, involved in what was going on, yet not quite in it.

The next day, amid scenes of indescribable noise and tension, the decisive vote was taken. Despite the pleas for mercy, despite the organized efforts of Paine and the Girondins, the Convention voted to execute the deposed King as a traitor to France. On January 21, 1793, as thousands of Parisians crowded into the Place de la Révolution, Louis was led to the guillotine. Paine witnessed this event with growing dread, and now, for the first time in his life, a small doubt entered his mind. Perhaps men were not altogether reasonable animals and history was not marching strictly according to plan. The events that followed in 1793 confirmed this doubt and shook Paine's confidence in his life mission as violently as his experiences in 1792 had brought his confidence to a high pitch.

With the death of the King, the position of the Girondins became more difficult. Their speeches at the Convention were greeted with a steadily increasing barrage of hoots and catcalls from galleries packed with Jacobin sympathizers. The armies of several European countries, financed by the English and officered in part by French émigrés, invaded France anew and threatened the Revolution. Republican armies, rallying to the cry of Liberty, Fraternity, and Equality, spurred by the Marseillaise, the famous anthem composed at this time, resisted in a series of fierce battles near the frontier. In the spring General Dumouriez, the hero of Valmy, deserted to the invaders, and set up a wave of panic in Paris. The Jacobins proved more skillful at exploiting the panic than the Girondins; their superiority in political propaganda was in the end the weapon that brought them to absolute power. Under the prodding of Marat, the Convention appointed a Committee of Public Safety and gave it extraordinary powers to arrest and imprison anyone suspected of sympathizing with the foreign enemy. The Committee was packed with Jacobins, and in a short while it became a kind of government within the government.

Threatened by the Committee, badgered at the Convention, confused by the swift rush of events, the Girondins as a party gradually disintegrated during the spring of 1793. One of their principal leaders, Danton, seeing how the wind was blowing, deserted to the Jacobins. Those who remained behind felt themselves drowning in the political stream, and gave way to despair. Paine was caught up in the same whirlpool. His stout morale and optimism, powerful until now, began giving way.

He hated the Jacobins and what they stood for, recognized in them the pure lust for power, and was well aware of the corruption the greed for power brought with it. Yet he felt helpless to keep together the disintegrating Girondin cause. His ignorance of French was a particularly severe handicap at this time, keeping him out of touch with the swaying and shifting of the public temper and preventing his speeches at the Convention from having the impact of personal delivery.

Arrests grew more frequent, and the guillotine busier. The Committee of Public Safety, with war coming closer to Paris, became more ruthless in pursuit of the liberals and moderates. Paine devoted less of his energies to fighting parliamentary battles at the Convention and more to rescuing individual Englishmen and Americans from Jacobin wrath.

His zeal in this direction got him into trouble with the newly appointed American minister to France, his old enemy Gouverneur Morris. A number of American merchant ships carrying cargo to England had been captured by the French fleet in retaliation for the capturing of other American ships bound for France by the British fleet. The interned Americans sailors were clamoring to be released, but Morris, who was sympathetic to England and anxious for the French treaty with America to be broken, did nothing. As long as the Americans were detained on French soil, bad feeling would increase between America and France. When the sailors received no satisfaction from Morris, they appealed to Paine. He intervened on their behalf with Robespierre himself, arguing that their retention would damage the French cause in America. The seamen were freed, an act which caused Morris to hate Paine more bitterly than ever.

The repression continued at an increasing pace. In June, the Jacobins passed a bill expelling the Girondins from the Convention and outlawing them as a political party. In July, Marat was stabbed to death in his bathtub by Charlotte Corday, a peasant girl from Normandy—an event that encouraged the Jacobins to further assaults on their opponents. Paine, seeing the shadow of coming events, retired more and more from public life, and appeared at the Convention less and less often. It was at this time, out of a feeling of deep depression at the course of the Revolution, that Paine began drinking heavily in a vain attempt to drown his pessimism. But this phase soon passed. He went into a kind of semi-retirement from public life. Living off the proceeds of the farm at New Rochelle and occasional fees for newspaper articles, he began work on a book that had been simmering in his mind off and on for some years. He called it *The Age of Reason*. Dealing with religion, it was a book that would arouse a storm of enemies, and give him the mistaken and inaccurate reputation of atheist while he was still alive and for more than a century after his death.

With friends and associates being guillotined right and left, Paine retired more and more to his hotel room and worked on his new book. Early in October the last remaining group of Girondin leaders were imprisoned and on the last day of the month they were guillotined en masse. After this bloody event Paine was the only prominent anti-Jacobin left in the country outside of jail, and he knew that he would not be allowed to remain at liberty much longer. Only his standing and reputation in America had saved him thus far. When a decree was passed in November preventing aliens from holding public office and he thus lost his seat in the Convention, he knew that his free days were numbered. He plugged away steadily at *The Age of Reason* and finished it at last on the morning of December 28. By a dramatic coincidence, the order for his arrest was issued six hours later. When the police platoon knocked on his door, Paine was ready. He asked permission to turn the manuscript over to a friend. This was granted. Paine and the police went to the lodgings of Joel Barlow, a young American writer from Connecticut who admired Paine, and there *The Age of Reason* was delivered for safekeeping. Later that evening the grim doors of the Luxembourg Prison (successor to the Bastille) closed behind Paine, and his ten-month martyrdom began.

Barlow succeeded in getting *The Age of Reason* printed, and copies of the book began appearing in

America early in 1794. Paine dedicated his new work
TO MY FELLOW CITIZENS OF THE UNITED
STATES OF AMERICA:

> I put the following work under your protection
> [the dedication ran]. It contains my opinion upon
> religion. You will do me the justice to remember,
> that I have always strenuously supported the right
> of every man to his opinion, however different that
> opinion might be to mine. He who denies to another
> this right, makes a slave of himself to his present
> opinion, because he precludes himself the right of
> changing it.

The book itself was a long and detailed attack on the
Bible as the word of God. Paine refused to believe that
Moses received the Ten Commandents from Jehovah on
Mt. Sinai and he refused equally to believe in the divinity
of Christ. Christ was a great man with admirable opinions
but to accept the miracles surrounding him was more
than Reason would allow. Paine then classified all the
contradictory statements of the four books of the Gospel,
attacked all the vengeful and bloodthirsty events of the
Old Testament, and arrived at the conclusion that revealed religion, depending as it did on the testimony of
human beings who were of necessity merely mortal,
could not be taken as true. Moreover, other world reli-
gions aside from Judaism and Christianity claimed to have

direct messages from God. Which of them was right? Paine preferred to believe that all of them were wrong.

Did this mean, therefore, that God did not exist? Not at all. Paine began *The Age of Reason* by asserting His existence. "I believe in one God, and no more; and I hope for happiness beyond this life." He went on to define the acts of a religious man: "I believe that religious duties consist in doing justice, loving mercy, and endeavoring to make our fellow-creatures happy." As for proof that God exists: ". . . some, perhaps, will say: Are we to have no word of God—no revelation? I answer, Yes; there is a word of God; there is a revelation. The Word of God is the Creation we behold: and it is in this word, which no human invention can counterfeit or alter, that God speaketh universally to man."

Paine, like other eighteenth-century deists, believed strongly in Creation or Nature. The world of Nature was harmonious and orderly. It had its definite laws. It was beautiful. And all these qualities could be perceived at once by every observer. If Nature existed—and who could doubt that it did—God existed, too, as its Creator.

> The Creation . . . . is an ever-existing original, which every man can read. It cannot be forged; it cannot be counterfeited; it cannot be lost; it cannot be altered; it cannot be suppressed. It does not depend upon the will of man whether it shall be pub-

lished or not; it publishes itself from one end of the earth to the other. It preaches to all nations and to all worlds . . .

Paine then launched one of his eloquent flights of argument:

> Do we move to contemplate his power? We see it in the immensity of the Creation. Do we want to contemplate his wisdom? We see it in the unchangeable order by which the . . . whole is governed. Do we want to contemplate his munificence? We see it in the abundance with which he fills the earth. Do we want to contemplate his mercy? We see it in his not withholding that abundance even from the unthankful. In fine, do we want to know what God is? Search not the book called the Scripture, which any human hand might make, but the Scripture called the Creation.

As a product of the Enlightenment, that eighteenth-century movement which believed in the essential rationality and goodness of man, Paine could not resist referring to this goodness as a final proof of God's presence.

> . . . I totally disbelieve that the Almighty ever did communicate anything to man, by any mode of speech, in any language, or by any kind of vision, or appearance, or by any means which our senses are capable of receiving, otherwise than by the universal display of himself in the works of the crea-

tion, and by that repugnance we feel in ourselves to bad actions, and the disposition to do good ones.

The Age of Reason was not very impressive as Scriptural criticism. It was not particularly original in its conclusions. But it rose from the atmosphere of the time, and was perfectly consistent with Paine's ideas and ways of thinking. He looked upon the organized churches in England and France, based as they were on revealed religion, as the allies of the royalist governments of those countries. He had attacked the governments. It was logical that he should come to examine the religious institutions which supported them. Since these institutions derived their authority from the sanctity of the Scriptures, Paine in due course inspected the claims of this sanctity, and rejected them. Not from the point of view of an atheist or even an agnostic, but as a deist who inferred the existence of God from the direct evidence of senses and reason.

If the church had no valid supernatural claim, Paine argued, it had no right to be an official state religion, and the citizenry ought to be free to embrace it or not as they chose. The ferocious assaults on priests and church during the French Revolution had been preceded by the peaceful constitutional separation of church and state in America. It was the American example that Paine applauded and pointed to as ideal.

The uproar created by Paine's earlier writings was as

nothing to the storm aroused by *The Age of Reason*. In America, clergymen by the dozens raised an outcry against him as a blasphemer and anti-Christ. Since he refused to accept the divinity of Christ, they accused him—inaccurately—of being an atheist. His attack on the holiness of the Bible they regarded as a campaign against the most sacred feelings of Judeo-Christian civilization. Few things arouse men more than an attack on their religious convictions. The earlier charges against Paine were forgivable. The rumor that he was a drunkard, even when believed, was not very damaging in what was, after all, a hard-drinking time. The accusations that he was unkempt and shabbily dressed, or that he was an interfering foreigner, or that his father was not a gentleman, were taken seriously in some circles but had little effect on the mass of citizens.

The Age of Reason was another matter. It cut across social lines, and drove a spear not at governments and kings but at the intimate sentiments of ordinary men. The subject was a touchy one, which a prudent writer would have avoided altogether. This was the first book Paine wrote which was not in direct response to an immediately urgent situation. Unlike his earlier books, it had no audience waiting to be convinced. Paine was getting out of his system ideas that had been fermenting for years, but there was no particular emergency to which they were addressed. He had, then, everything to lose and little to gain by its publication, and everything was just about what he did lose. The accusations launched against him by the clergy and by devout laymen found a widespread acceptance. The great reputation, the immense store of good will Paine had left behind him in America began to melt under the charges of blasphemy. Federalist newspapers, influenced by the political hostility of Hamilton and Adams toward Paine, wrote editorials attacking the author of *Common Sense* as an irresponsible radical who would destroy church and state, and all other institutions that kept human society together. The popular press used more violent language to lampoon him, and printed abusive cartoons showing Paine, his face distorted in a snarl, setting fire to a church. No reputation could long survive such treatment. Paine left America in 1787 a hero. He was to return in 1802 something of a villain.

When *The Age of Reason* was published, Paine was already in prison, and heard nothing of the sound and fury it aroused. The Luxembourg was an ancient medieval pile of gray rock, damp and poorly lighted. In the winter a cold chill came out of the stone walls and hung in the cells day and night; in the summer the air turned steamy and dank. Prisons in the eighteenth century were designed for punishment and suffering, not for rehabilitation; they achieved their aim supremely. Not that this mattered much to the inmates of the Luxembourg in

1793 and 1794. Nearly all of them were temporary
residents. They were there for a few days or, at the most,
a few weeks, then were led to the guillotine. Paine's
cellmates changed constantly. He became friendly with
several of them, and grieved when they were taken away.
To avoid the soul-destroying boredom of prison confinement, Paine busied himself with writing a second part to
The Age of Reason, but there were long hours when he
sat staring into space, mourning over his shattered revolutionary dream.

When the news of Paine's imprisonment spread
through Paris, the Americans living there went in a body
to Gouverneur Morris and petitioned him, as the American minister, to secure the great patriot's release. Morris
stalled. He claimed that Paine had become a Frenchman
when he accepted membership in the National Convention. He raised other objections before consenting at last
to speak to the French foreign minister. But he informed
the French foreign minister that his government did not
feel responsible for Paine, and hinted broadly that the
French could do what they wished with him. Morris, a
natural conservative, hated the French Revolution and
all its works, but he hated Paine too, and had no objection to seeing one destroy the other. To Secretary of
State Jefferson he wrote in February 1794:

> Lest I forget it I must mention that Thomas Paine
> is in prison, where he amuses himself with publish-

ing a pamphlet against Jesus Christ. . . . I incline
to think that if he is quiet in prison he may have the
good luck to be forgotten, whereas should he be
brought much into notice, the long suspended axe
might fall on him. I believe he thinks I ought to
claim him as an American citizen; but, considering
his birth, his naturalization in this country, and the
place he filled, I doubt much the right, and I am
sure the claim would be, for the present, at least,
inexpedient and ineffectual.

No move was made. Jefferson, thus advised by the
American representative on the scene, reasoned that
Paine's best chance was to lie low, that if America made
an official demand the French might execute him on the
spot by way of demonstrating their freedom from foreign interference. President Washington, in whom *The
Age of Reason* had aroused an acute distaste, agreed.
Nothing, then, was done. Morris had his way. The peti-
tioning Americans in Paris were outraged but helpless.
Paine, when he heard the news, became almost ill with
bitterness, a bitterness directed mainly at Washington.
He felt that never had a man been more shamefully abandoned by a wartime comrade, or more cruelly abandoned
by the country he helped create.

The Reign of Terror, in the meanwhile, went on without letup, and now began to devour its makers. In the
spring of 1794, Danton was overthrown, imprisoned
briefly at the Luxembourg, and then guillotined. In July

Robespierre himself suffered the same fate, while the Terror entered its final convulsive spasms. Paine was one of the few long-term prisoners. Being a foreigner and an American (at least unofficially), he was regarded as a special case by the Jacobins who, when they thought about him at all in the fierce tempo of revolutionary politics, had trouble arriving at a decision. Finally, in June, a decision was reached. Robespierre (a month before his own arrest) signed a warrant for Paine's death. In a letter written much later Paine described what followed:

> One hundred and sixty-eight persons were taken out of the Luxembourg in one night, and one hundred and sixty of them guillotined the next day, of which I knew I was to be one; and the manner I escaped that fate is curious, and has all the appearance of accident. The room in which I lodged was on the ground floor, one of a long range under a gallery, and the door opened outward and flat against the wall . . . When persons by scores and hundreds were taken out for the guillotine it was always done by night, and those who performed that office had a private mark or sign by which they knew what rooms to go to and what number to take. We were four, and the door of our room was marked, unobserved by us, with that number, in chalk; but it happened, if happening is the proper word, that the door was open and flat against the wall, and thereby

the mark came inside when we shut it at night; and
the destroying angel passed by.

Having been rescued miraculously—though this is
hardly the word the author of *The Age of Reason* would
have used—Paine continued to enjoy a run of luck. Before another warrant could be issued, Robespierre was
overthrown, and the immediate danger to Paine's life
passed.

He was fifty-seven when the doors of the great gray
prison on the Left Bank closed behind him. The ordeal
of prison life, the tensions of his narrow escape from
death, ate steadily into his health. He developed an abscess in his side, which stubbornly refused to heal. His
face aged visibly and developed deep lines. His hair
whitened. Only an uncommonly robust constitution
enabled him to survive at all.

Paine could almost tell what was happening in the
world outside by the coming and going of the prisoners;
they supplied him with news which allowed him to reg-
ister the feverish course of the Terror. Having opposed
it from the start and been thrust into a dungeon by it, he
could now only count its swelling roll of victims and
await its inevitable end. Liberty, Fraternity, Equality
were grim echoes from a remote past, and rang hollowly
through the corridors of the Luxembourg.

The execution of Robespierre was followed a month

later by the end of Morris' term as American minister to France—another stroke of good fortune for Paine. The new minister was James Monroe, who would one day be the fifth President of the United States and the author of the Monroe Doctrine. Paine and Monroe had been friends during the Revolutionary War, and Monroe, on arriving in Paris, was shocked to discover that Paine was still in prison. He sent a letter to Paine assuring him of his good wishes, then hurried to the French government and claimed Paine as an American citizen who had been arrested on no specified charge and whose immediate release would give great pleasure and relief to his country. In another letter to Paine he wrote: "It is unnecessary for me to tell you how much all of your countrymen . . . are interested in your welfare. They have not forgotten the history of their own revolution . . . nor the merits of those who served them in that great conflict."

But there were delays. The Committee of General Security, cleaning up in the wake of Robespierre, was reluctant to move fast. Morris remained in Paris through October and used his influence to keep his old enemy in jail. A vague statement was issued saying that though an American citizen, Paine was still liable for violation of French laws. Monroe acknowledged the truth of this in a letter to the Committee at the beginning of November, and then went on to state: "The citizens of the United

States can never look back to the era of their own revolution, without remembering . . . the name of Thomas Paine. The services which he rendered them in their struggle for liberty have made an impression of gratitude which will never be erased. . . . He is now in prison, languishing under a disease, and which must be increased by his confinement. Permit me, then, to call your attention, and to require that you will hasten his trial in case there be any charge against him, and if there be none, that you will cause him to be set at liberty."

At long last, on November 6, the order for Paine's release reached Monroe. He hurried down to the Luxembourg with it himself to expedite matters. Paine's shrunken and haggard appearance shocked him. He summoned a carriage, and the two men rode to Monroe's house on the Rue de Clichy where Paine was to stay and recover his health. It was more than ten months since Paine had breathed fresh air and seen, outdoors, the light of day. In that time a whole era had come to an end in France, while Paine himself had become an old man. The revolutionary flame burned in him still but no longer as ardently or as hotly as before; it had been chilled considerably by the course of the French Revolution.

With the fall of the Jacobins, the Convention had fallen into the hands of sober, hardheaded bureaucrats who had had enough of fanatical idealism, of terror, and of the insecurity of a police state. They sought, by negotiation, to put an end to the invasion of France by various European armies; and they strove to temper the mob at home by mild reforms. This was the period of the First and Second Directory, named after the committees of men who were now ruling France. Neither Directory was a success, and both were only to pave the way for the dictatorship of Napoleon, but they did abolish the more extreme forms of violence. They expressed the general desire to relax after the excesses of the Terror.

The new Convention was eager to restore Paine to his seat, and make up for his unjust imprisonment. The perennial business of drawing up a new constitution was still going on, and Paine was invited to take part. He accepted in principle and made one final appearance before the legislative body. His farewell speech was a plea to enfranchise the whole population, and to base the constitution on the whole people, excluding none from taking part in political life. This speech had no more actual effect than his plea to spare the life of Louis XVI, before the beginning of the Terror. His health and his optimism about the future of France had declined in about equal measure. At any rate, the Convention saw him no more. Paine withdrew, hoping to regain his health and return to America.

For some months after leaving prison his condition grew worse, and at one point early in 1795 the Monroes despaired of his life. Then he began to improve slowly.

In the meanwhile, he was making himself useful to Monroe as a political adviser. The policy of the Washington administration was to get closer to England, France's deadly enemy—a policy which meant estrangement between France and America. Monroe's own sympathies were with the French, as of course were Paine's, and Monroe was called upon several times to reassure the French about his country's negotiations with England.

Even when John Jay, notoriously conservative and anti-French in his sympathies, was sent to England to negotiate a treaty, Monroe continued to assure the French that all would be well. But when the Jay Treaty was announced in March 1795, Monroe felt betrayed and the French were furious. For in the treaty America permitted England to continue her practice of stopping American ships on the high seas and removing cargo sent from any country with which England was at war. This meant that though America claimed neutrality in the European conflict, she was allowing England to cut off all trade between herself and France, thus violating the traditional freedom of the seas.

Paine's anger at Washington now reached a boil, and spilled over in a letter he composed to the first President on his birthday, February 22, 1795.

> . . . it is not without some difficulty that I have taken the resolution to write to you. The danger to which I have been exposed cannot have been un-

known to you, and the guarded silence you have observed upon that circumstance, is what I ought not have expected from you, either as a friend or as a President of the United States.

He went on to accuse Washington of deserting him in his hour of need:

You knew enough of my character to be assured that I could not have deserved imprisonment in France. . . . But I cannot find that you so much as directed any enquiry to be made whether I was in prison or at liberty, dead or alive; what the cause of that imprisonment was, or whether there was any service or assistance you could render. Is this what I ought to have expected from America after the part I have acted towards her?

And in an increasingly bitter tone he continued:

I do not hesitate to say that you have not served America with . . . greater zeal, or more fidelity, than myself . . . After the revolution of America was established, you rested at home to partake its advantages, and I ventured into new scenes of difficulty to extend the principles which that revolution had produced. In the progress of events you beheld yourself a president in America and me a prisoner in France: you folded your arms, forgot your friend, and became silent.

Paine still hoped for some explanation, some word from Washington that might clear the air. Monroe begged Paine not to send the letter, arguing that it would do Washington no good and Paine much harm, that while some of the charges might be true, Paine was certainly unjust in accusing Washington of taking an easy path by staying at home after the Revolution. Surely Paine must realize that being President was no easy task, that the interests of the country sometimes required that personal sentiment be put aside. Paine didn't agree with these arguments, but didn't wish to embarrass Monroe, who was, after all, the American minister to France and in whose house (the official property of the United States) he was staying. He therefore did not send the letter, but waited, hoping that he would hear from Washington anyway.

The spring and summer of 1795 passed without a word from the President. Paine's abscess grew worse, his mood more bitter. He continued to brood over the injustice and ill treatment he felt himself to be suffering at the hands of his country, and in September he drafted another letter to Washington in which he repeated much that he had said in the earlier one. He asked for proof that Washington had not conspired with Morris to get him jailed in the first place, and as good as charged the President not simply with ingratitude but with personal treachery. This letter he did send, and like earlier communications and complaints, it was greeted with dead silence.

The winter of 1795–96 saw a slow improvement in Paine's health but none in his feelings toward Washington. He finally grew well enough to leave the Monroes and resume living in his own lodgings. He took leave of these devoted friends with warm expressions of gratitude. There was no doubt in his mind that Monroe had saved his life, just as there was no longer any doubt in his mind that Washington would have been willing to see him lose it. Almost a year after his last letter was sent, Paine, on July 30, 1796, published his *Letter to George Washington*, which brought into the open his long-pent-up passions on the subject. The *Letter* went over much of the ground Paine had already put down in his private correspondence, and attacked the pro-British, anti-French policy of the Washington administration. This, Paine charged in a series of climactic paragraphs, constituted a betrayal of the principles for which the American Revolution was fought.

Like all of Paine's published writings, this one aroused strong passions in the United States. Domestic sentiment was by no means entirely favorable to Washington. The Jay Treaty was intensely unpopular in many quarters, and Jay himself had been burned in effigy in demonstrations against it. The President was still suspected of royalist sympathies, and closer ties with England at the expense of France did not sit too well with a people that still remembered the bloody war for independence. The feeling of reverence for the father of his country, which was to settle upon America in later years, had not yet crystallized. Enough of it was present, however, to arouse violent indignation against Paine's *Letter*. Those who were already distrustful of him as a result of his attack on organized religion in *The Age of Reason* found in his attack on Washington final cause for regarding Paine as the devil's agent.

Perhaps the man least aroused by the uproar was the target of it—Washington himself. By disposition cold, by manners retiring, the great general was the most self-sufficient of men. Deeply moved by a sense of duty, he cared little for social contacts and was largely indifferent to public opinion. He had fought under the British in the French and Indian War and had lived as an English gentleman in Virginia. But when circumstances called for it, he had led a rebel American army against British rule. After the war, he had reverted to his natural sympathies with the mother country, to whom he always felt much closer than he did to France. His convictions were aristocratic rather than democratic, and Paine's ideas about repudiating the past, the equality of men, the vote for everyone, the rule of the people, the reactionary role of the church, were peculiarly distasteful to him. He resented having *The Rights of Man* dedicated to him, and had sent Morris to France as the American envoy because Morris, like himself, was unsympathetic to the

French Revolution. Morris' argument that Paine was safer in prison than out of it had seemed to him perfectly sound. He had no wish to see Paine die but he was not as concerned for his personal safety as he would have been in 1783 when their wartime friendship was at its height.

One of Washington's great achievements was his ability to work with men who had been his enemies, and getting men with opposing ideas to work together under him. John Adams had been among those who in 1777 had wanted to fire Washington as commander-in-chief on the grounds of military incompetence. (Ironically, Paine had successfully defended Washington on that occasion.) Yet he was now Vice President and one of Washington's closest supporters. Hamilton and Jefferson, brilliant men and deadly enemies, were both members of the same cabinet. Washington was undoubtedly the only man who could have persuaded these two to work together for the good of the country. Edmund Randolph, the Attorney General, often spoke of Washington's genius for conciliation, his ability to put principle and duty above personal likes and dislikes.

The *Letter to George Washington* broke the last tie between the two men. The sword and pen of the Revolution, as they had been called, were now irreconcilable. All the circles sympathetic to the President were closed to Paine. And even those who were not partial to Washington felt somehow that Paine should not have made his quarrel public, or at least not have assaulted the President in such violent terms. All things considered, Monroe had been right in advising Paine not to publish the letter. Though it gave Paine an outlet for his outraged feelings, it made him many more enemies than friends, and did no public good. In this instance, Monroe proved himself a much more effective apostle of reason than Paine himself, who tried so hard to make reason an honored faculty among men.

In 1796 America's third Presidential election took place. John Adams succeeded Washington (who had refused a third term), defeating Jefferson for the office, and guaranteeing the continuation of the pro-British, anti-French policies of the federal government. Monroe was recalled as minister to France and replaced by Charles Pinckney, a man so hostile to the French Republic that the French Council of Ministers refused to receive him. The Monroes, packing to go home, asked Paine to accompany them. He had been away from his own country long enough. Surely, they urged, it was time for him to return. Paine agreed, and traveled with the Monroes to Havre. In the Channel he could see British frigates just outside French territorial waters. The Jay Treaty had allowed them to continue intercepting neutral ships and removing from them persons hostile to England. Since

Paine was still Public Enemy No. 1 to the Pitt regime, he would have been a great prize. Paine had no intention of spending the rest of his days in an English dungeon, having just been released from a French one.

He reluctantly parted company with the Monroes, and returned to Paris.

RETURN TO AMERICA

WHEN Paine got back to the French capital, he was convinced that his stay would be temporary. As soon as a peace treaty was signed with England, the blockade would be lifted and he would be free to go. Meanwhile, he took up lodgings with an old political associate from the early days of the Revolution, Nicholas Bonneville, now the editor of a liberal republican newspaper critical of the Directory. Mme. Bonneville, a round-faced jolly woman with three children and no great passion for housekeeping, made him welcome too, and he settled down to a somewhat untidy domestic comfort much as he had had with the Rickman family in London.

The year before, he had written the rough draft of a pamphlet called *Agrarian Justice*, to which he now put the finishing touches. Late in 1796, as a protest against the poverty that still existed in France despite the overthrow of the aristocracy, a violent uprising against the complacent Directory took place under the journalist Babeuf, whose followers were inspired by the teachings of Marat. The uprising was suppressed bloodily; the extremes of wealth and poverty which gave rise to it continued to exist. It was this problem that Paine tackled in his pamphlet.

In it he made another of his original proposals that has since been generally adopted: government subsidies and old-age pensions. Still in the vein of *The Age of Reason*, he began by making a characteristic comment:

> It is wrong to say God made *rich* and *poor;* He made only *male* and *female;* and He gave them the earth for their inheritance. . . . Practical religion consists in doing good: and the only way of serving God is that of endeavoring to make His Creation happy. All preaching that has not this for its object is nonsense and hypocrisy.

The earth, argued Paine, belongs to the whole community, and only the improvement made by cultivation belongs to the individual who makes it.

> Every proprietor . . . of cultivated lands owes to the community a *ground-rent* (for I know no better term to express the idea) for the land which he holds. . . .
> There could be no such thing as landed property originally. Man did not make the earth, and though he had a natural right to *occupy* it, he had no right to *locate as his property* . . . any part of it; neither did the Creator of the earth open a land-office, from whence the first title-deeds should issue.

The ground-rent would be paid into a large public fund. From this fund, proposed Paine, every young man would be given fifteen pounds when he reached the age of twenty-one, and every person over fifty would be granted a pension of ten pounds a year. By encouraging the young and protecting the old, by siphoning off some of the excess from the swollen coffers of the rich and distributing it among the rest of the population, society would become more just.

> It is not charity but a right, not bounty but justice, that I am pleading for. The present state of civilization is as odious as it is unjust. It is absolutely the opposite of what it should be, and it is necessary that

a revolution should be made in it. The contrast of affluence and wretchedness continually meeting and offending the eye, is like dead and living bodies chained together.

And he wound up with another of his striking affirmations about ideas being more powerful than swords.

An army of principles will penetrate where an army of soldiers cannot; it will succeed where diplomatic management would fail; it is neither the Rhine, the Channel, nor the ocean that can arrest its progress: it will march on the horizon of the world, and it will conquer.

Agrarian Justice marked Paine's switch in interest from politics to economics, from social institutions to the operations of money. Money, he realized, was the key to the new age. The end of Bourbon feudalism meant the beginning of the Industrial Revolution, and with it the era of machinery and finance. Henceforth, Paine's European writing was devoted to budgets, currency, taxes, and stock-market speculations. On nearly all these subjects, he was to have something unique to say, always within the framework of his vision of a better world.

While he waited for safe passage home, he resumed his old interest in mechanical and scientific inventions. His iron bridge had finally been built across the river Wear in Sunderland, England, but as a fugitive from England, with a warrant still out for his arrest, Paine no longer had any connection with the bridge and received no money for it. In Paris he fitted out a workshop in the Bonnevilles' cellar, and there banged away at new experiments. He blew off many a firecracker in an attempt to use gunpowder instead of steam as a form of fuel, and had long discussions with Robert Fulton, then busy launching a steamboat on the Seine, on the subject of steam-driven navigation. He built an advanced type of crane, developed a machine for planing boards, and puttered about with various kinds of wheels.

But he always returned to his first love, the bridge. He began making a great number of improved models, some of pasteboard, some of lead. "I shall bring these models with me when I come home," he wrote to Thomas Jefferson in 1800, "which will be as soon as I can pass the seas in safety from the piratical John Bulls." In the meantime, while waiting for the John Bulls to withdraw, he worked to all hours at his inventions. Often, when achieving some long sought-after success, he would wake the Bonnevilles in the middle of the night, hustle them into his study, and burst out in explosions of gratified vanity. The eighteenth century—the century of the Enlightenment—produced that peculiar and remarkable human type, the scientist-philosopher, of whom, among Americans, Franklin, Jefferson, and Paine were celebrated examples.

In politics, he exerted all his efforts at reducing tension

between France and America, and preventing war between the two countries—an unthinkable prospect a few short years before. The famous Talleyrand was now the French foreign minister, and a good deal of hocus-pocus went on behind the scenes, involving graft, national interests, and jockeying for position and power. These affairs, tangled in intrigue, kept the issues of war and peace hanging in the balance through the first two years of President Adams' tenure; there was even some skirmishing at sea between French and American warships. Paine's prestige with the French continued strong. Though he did not like the Directory's lack of ardor for reform, he supported it anyway as the inheritor of the Revolution, and intervened with the Directors time and again to assure them of America's essentially good intentions. By the end of 1798 the crisis was resolved when Adams withdrew Pinckney and appointed an American minister sympathetic to the French.

In 1798 a new and spectacular figure had appeared upon the scene—Napoleon Bonaparte—whom Paine was to meet at close range and who was to shake the world. Troops under his leadership had put down a royalist uprising in 1795. "A whiff of grapeshot is all that's needed," Napoleon is reported to have said, a simple remedy for political trouble that turned out to be the cornerstone of his career. In 1797 he had invaded Italy at the head of a French army and won a series of striking victories over mixed Austrian and Italian troops. On his return he was acclaimed as a hero.

It was at the end of the Italian campaign that Napoleon paid the first of his visits to Paine. He called at the Bonneville house, No. 4 Rue du Théâtre-Français, and began heaping praise on the aging writer. A gold statue should be erected to Thomas Paine in every city in the world, he exclaimed. He, General Bonaparte, slept every night with *The Rights of Man* under his pillow, and knew *Common Sense* and *The Age of Reason* practically word for word. Paine was a guiding star for all true idealists and republicans. Warm words and lavish compliments poured in a steady stream from the short, stocky, energetic Corsican. He turned the full force and charm of his personality on Paine. This was the period when Napoleon was cultivating all the philosophers and scientists in Paris, advertising himself as the man who would spread the ideals of the French Revolution. Eighteen years later, at Waterloo, Liberty, Fraternity, and Equality were popular slogans still, but they were stacked grotesquely on the ten million European dead, the price paid for Napoleon's dream of world conquest.

Paine was much taken with the little general. What man was not? When he made the effort, Bonaparte could convince even the most hardened skeptic of his sincerity. Besides, Paine was flattered. Where his ideas were concerned, Paine had a more than normal share of vanity

and liked nothing better than to stand as master to disciple. And here was a disciple who, at twenty-eight, had
already fired the imagination of the whole country. Later
visits confirmed the first favorable impression, and Paine's
interest in French politics revived.

Late in 1798 the Directory, at Napoleon's suggestion,
drew up plans for the invasion of England, a scheme in
which Paine was invited to take part. Napoleon, knowing Paine's feelings about the English government, hoped
for his strong support. Paine was not against the idea of
an invasion if it meant replacing the British monarchy
with a republic. But he had no illusions about the success
of such an expedition. Napoleon was certain that the
English people would rise up against their rulers and support the French. Paine was certain they would not. He
detested the policies of the Pitt regime, but he knew his
own countrymen well enough to say they would support
the worst government in the world if it rallied them
against invasion from abroad.

Napoleon was greatly displeased. He had cultivated
Paine to win his support in exactly such a situation, and
now the old fool was opposing him. The argument grew
furious, but the enthusiasm of the Directors had been
dampened and the invasion project was abandoned. Napoleon revived it ten years later when England, alone
among the countries of Europe, continued to hold out
against him. He actually began building a fleet of invasion

barges at Boulogne. But the British fleet, under Nelson, had already defeated the French and their allies in a series of naval engagements, and in the end proved too large an obstacle. Napoleon gave up invasion again and went back to the old Directory idea of cutting off British trade with the rest of the world by an organized boycott.

After their dispute, Napoleon never again spoke to Paine, and referred to him on a later occasion "as a rascal, like the rest of the English." A year later he overthrew the Directory and replaced it with a committee of three consuls, of which he was the First. Soon, the other two consuls disappeared, and First Consul Bonaparte presently evolved into Emperor Napoleon I. While still using the slogans of the Revolution for all they were worth, he installed a rigid press censorship. Bonneville, who ran a newspaper aptly named *Le Bien Informé*, was thrown into jail for criticizing the new Caesar, and though he was soon released, his paper was banned permanently. By this time Paine himself was thoroughly against Bonaparte, in whom he saw a cynical and unscrupulous exploiter of men's hopes for a new and better society. With this disillusionment, his disgust with French politics, indeed with the politics of Europe altogether, became complete. As the new century dawned, Paine began longing more than ever for America and the remembered freshness of the New World.

His relations with the Bonnevilles were very close.

The careless informality with which Mme. Bonneville ran the house suited him perfectly, tidiness not being one of the virtues he admired. He enjoyed the company of the three children, the second of whom bore his name. As with the Rickmans, the French family supplied him with warm domestic ties. In exchange for room and board, he turned over to the Bonnevilles the small income from his property in America, wrote extensively for *Le Bien Informé* as long as it appeared, and helped with Bonneville's other literary enterprises. His hosts did not suffer financially from these arrangements but in any event, they would have been glad to support Paine for nothing. Bonneville had published the French translation of *The Rights of Man*, and in his eyes Paine was a great man whose presence honored his house. The parade of celebrities who came to pay their respects kept Mme. Bonneville in a state of pleased agitation and excitement. The appearance of General Bonaparte alone, and the courtly grace with which he greeted her, left her in a glow for days.

The long wait continued. The nineteenth century arrived, and with it the election of Thomas Jefferson as third President of the United States. This event, which filled Paine with joy, filled him also with a renewed passion for home. The ill fortune that overtook the Bonnevilles made life with them less agreeable; after the suppression of his paper, Bonneville found it increasingly

difficult to earn a living. Paine worried over their growing poverty and urged them to emigrate to America. He
spent less of his time at home and more in shabby taverns
and cafés frequented by Irish and Polish revolutionaries,
hotheaded exiles from embattled and occupied countries.
He would entertain his friends for hours with anecdotes
of the Revolutionary War and burst into harangues on
his favorite subjects at that time, religion and Bonaparte.
People who met him during this period spoke of his
vigor, the clarity and power of his mind, and the moodi-
ness which would seize him frequently and cause him to
sink suddenly into melancholy silences.

Jefferson, with whom he corresponded irregularly,
knew of his state and was eager for Paine to return. In
1801 he invited Paine to come back on the American
frigate *Maryland*, as an official guest of the government.
"I am in hopes," the President remarked in his letter of
invitation, "you will find us returned . . . to sentiments worthy of former times. In these it will be your
glory to have steadily labored, and with as much effect as
any man living. That you may long live to continue your
useful labors and to reap the reward in the thankfulness
of nations, is my sincere prayer." When Jefferson's enemies among the Federalists got wind of the offer, they
raised a terrific hubbub. What? Escort to America at
public expense a dangerous radical, an enemy of religion,
an ill-mannered drunkard? Outrageous. The followers

of Hamilton looked upon Jefferson's election as ushering in "the rule of the mob," and his gesture to Paine confirmed it in their eyes. To spare his friend political embarrassment, Paine declined the invitation, and stayed on in France.

It was, in the end, Bonaparte who came to his rescue—unintentionally, of course. The First Consul, anxious for a period of peace to consolidate his power at home and already thinking of crowning himself emperor, embarked on a series of treaties with the principal European powers. The last of these was England, and the Treaty of Amiens, signed in March 1802, brought war between the two bitter enemies to a temporary halt. British cruisers hovering outside French ports withdrew. The blockade was lifted. Paine was now free to leave.

But news traveled slowly in those days. Before word reached Paris, before the British officially proclaimed their withdrawal, before Paine could secure passage, some months passed. At last he packed his bags, bade farewell to the Bonnevilles, urging them to follow him to America, and set off by coach for Havre. His old friend Thomas Rickman had come over from London to see him off. The two men had a warm reunion, and on September 1, 1802, Rickman waved farewell to the vessel carrying Paine homeward to America.

The fifteen years of his absence were momentous in the history of the country he did so much to found. After years of debate the Constitution had been adopted. The conservative administrations of Washington and Adams had been followed by the liberal regime of Jefferson. The urge for expansion westward had already become strong; indeed one of the provisions of the hotly disputed Jay Treaty was the evacuation by the British of certain western forts. The country had passed through a civil liberties crisis with the Alien and Sedition Laws of 1798, which provided jail terms for anyone criticizing a public officer; after three years these laws had been repealed. The slave trade was soon to be banned, but the slave system had already grown firmly entrenched in the South.

The greatest change of all was psychological. A whole generation had passed since the War for Independence, and the memories of that crucial conflict had begun to fade. Its heroes were no longer quite so vivid in the public mind, and the sense of unity—always stronger in war than in peace—had crumbled under the pressure of conflicting interests. Men were struggling, not to be born as a nation or to survive as one, but for personal gain and advancement; the ordinary selfishness of everyday life had replaced the idealistic ends of patriotism, self-sacrifice, and the national interest. Another emergency would rouse the Americans to further unity and common effort. But at the moment there was no emergency. Times were relatively "normal." Firebrands from the earlier period no longer enjoyed their former prestige.

This was especially true of Paine, who had been out of the country altogether, out of personal touch with the new generation that had grown up in the meanwhile. Many younger Americans, if they knew of him at all, knew of him only as an "irresponsible radical" or a "dangerous atheist"—the caricatures spread around his name by an unfriendly press.

After a two-month ocean voyage Paine landed at Baltimore on October 31, 1802. The old war horse had at last come home, but there was no war. The author of the *Crisis* papers found a nation busily engaged in expansion and trade, but there was no overwhelming crisis to command his energies anew. His career had been a series of responses to great emergencies; the next great emergency in America was not to arise until the War of 1812. At peace, America was far from the country he had first come to in 1774. This new America had lost its revolutionary ardor and assumed a workaday air. Its heroes were merchants and landowners, not reformers or idealists. In this changed society, Paine was to find himself emotionally unemployed. He was not to blame for the situation. But then neither was America. It is natural, indeed inevitable, that nations, like men, live on a routine level unless forced by pressure to live intensely and dramatically.

Paine's was a nature geared to pressure, a mind that flourished best in time of tension. When the times were ordinary, rather than extraordinary, his richest qualities tended to be hidden. Had he first arrived in America as a young man in 1802, it seems likely that he would never have been heard from. Arriving as he did at a critical moment, he was thrust into prominence by the revolutionary explosion he himself had helped touch off.

The actual Paine who at the age of sixty-five landed at Baltimore had no thoughts of fame and glory. His main idea was to spend his declining years in the friendly and congenial atmosphere of the nation he helped create. He was old; he was tired. While not really ill, he was not entirely well, and would never recover fully from the effects of his imprisonment. The last years in France, what with the hard times that overtook the Bonnevilles and friction with Napoleon, had been trying ones. The desire for rest, for peace, even for the rest and peace of obscurity, was very strong in him. Had he been allowed to live in quiet retirement, he might have been entirely content. He had close friends still, particularly Colonel Kirkbride, who urged him to take up residence again in Bordentown, New Jersey. Or there was the large and fertile farm at New Rochelle—surely an ideal place to retire in. With the exhausting pressures of Europe behind him, Paine watched the coastline of America slowly appear on the horizon, no longer with the eyes of a young man searching for adventure and opportunity but with the eyes of an old warrior longing for the quiet of home.

LAST YEARS
OF A
UNIVERSAL MAN

Peace and quiet had never been Tom Paine's lot in life, and they were not now.

News of his return had preceded him, and there were sneering, harshly critical articles about him in New York, Philadelphia and Baltimore newspapers, especially those hostile to President Jefferson. Many a preacher denounced him from the Sunday pulpit. His reception was something less than that accorded to a returning hero.

From Baltimore he sent his bridge models on ahead to

Jefferson, whose strong interest in inventions of all kinds was already well known. After resting for a few days from the long ocean voyage, Paine traveled down to Washington himself and put up at Lovell's Hotel. The Federalist Party was the chief opponent of Jefferson's Republicans, and its press let fly at Paine with both barrels. They described him as a "lying, drunken, brutal infidel," "the loathsome Thomas Paine, a drunken atheist," "Let Jefferson and his blasphemous crony dangle from the same gallows." The press in those days was truly "free." It could recommend that the President of the United States be hanged, with no fear of restraint. And this was only the beginning. Later, the newspapers described Paine as a "loathsome reptile," a "demi-human arch-beast," "an object of disgust, of abhorrence, of absolute loathing, to every decent man except the President of the United States."

President Jefferson, accustomed for many years to violent attacks and personal insults, paid little attention. He invited Paine to the Executive Mansion (it wasn't called the White House until Theodore Roosevelt gave it that name a hundred years later), where for two weeks he was an honored guest. The two men were seen walking together through the streets of Washington engaged in close and intimate conversation. Jefferson offered his friend a post in the government, which Paine refused, again out of fear of embarrassing the President by presenting his enemies with an official target that could be attacked day after day.

While Jefferson ignored the criticism, Paine was roused to counterattack. He was never one for taking things lying down, and even now in his old age, he found the energy to strike back at his vilifiers. He began issuing a series of essays called *Letters to the Citizens of the United States* in which he hacked away at the charges against him, ridiculed the Federalists, and reasserted his own principles. In *Letter I* he reintroduced himself to the American people: "After an absence of almost fifteen years, I am again returned to the country in whose dangers I bore my share, and to whose greatness I contributed my part." He leaped at once into his running quarrel with the Federalists whom he described as a "faction in the agonies of death," gnashing its teeth and struggling "in proportion as its fate approaches."

Letter II denied the Federalists' claim that they were the first advocates of a national government. Paine reserved this claim to himself: "I ought to stand first on the list of Federalists, for the proposition for establishing a general government over the Union came originally from me in 1783." It was not just a strong central government that the Federalists favored, Paine went on to charge, but they leaned secretly toward monarchy. Ex-President John Adams, one of their leaders, was "as full of kings, queens, and knaves, as a pack of cards,"

Paine commented stingingly. The Federalists replied in kind, and there was a merry row between the two sides. The noise, the angry tempers, the mud-slinging, the hubbub, the outpouring of biting words, continued without letup.

In *Letter III* Paine returned to the two subjects which made him most unpopular, in which he had the fewest supporters: George Washington and organized religion. He repeated his already published charges against Washington, and concluded bitterly: "He accepted as a present a hundred thousand acres in America, and left me to occupy six foot of earth in France." But Washington, who had died in 1799, had already become a national hero. His birthday was observed by both parties. Even the Republicans were embarrassed by Paine's attitude and remained silent when the Federalists denounced him for it.

Adding fuel to the fire in the same letter, Paine resumed his criticism of Christianity and his defense of deism. This was an even touchier matter than the memory of Washington. It offended the sensibilities of even those Americans who were not themselves religiously inclined, and was considered politically unwise by many Jeffersonians who in private shared the same views. Friends warned Paine that such sentiments would ruin his reputation. He brushed off the warnings. He was not, he said, a politician running for office, but a philosopher searching for truth, and in any case expressing sincere convictions. He recalled that people had warned him in 1776 not to talk about Independence on grave penalty of being jailed by the authorities. But he had gone on talking, and history had proved him right.

In *Letter IV* he stated: "In taking up any public matter, I have never made it a consideration, and never will, whether it be popular or unpopular; but whether it be *right* or *wrong*." One of his old friends, Sam Adams of Boston (cousin of the ex-President and famous for his role in the Boston Tea Party), took issue with him on his religious ideas, though he had supported Paine through thick and thin on everything else: "I have frequently with pleasure reflected on your services to my native and your adopted country. Your *Common Sense* and your *Crisis* unquestionably awakened the public mind and led the people loudly to call for a Declaration of our national Independence. I therefore esteemed you as a warm friend to the liberty and lasting welfare of the human race." He then proceeded to chide Paine for his attacks on the Bible, a book on which Adams had been brought up and held to be sacred.

Paine's reply was gentle, courteous, and firm. "If I do not believe as you believe," he wrote to Adams, "it proves that you do not believe as I believe, and this is all that it proves." A man is responsible for his theology not to his fellow men but to the Creator, or to Nature's God as He is called in the first sentence of the Declaration of Independence (a typical deistic term, Paine might have added slyly). "The key of heaven," ran the last paragraph of the letter to Adams, "is not in the keeping of any sect, nor ought the road to it be obstructed by any. Our relation to each other in this World is as Men, and the Man who is a friend to Man and to his rights, let his religious opinions be what they may, is a good citizen, to whom I can give, as I ought to do, and every other ought, the right hand of fellowship, and to none with more hearty good-will, my dear friend, than to you."

His personal relations with Jefferson continued undisturbed, as did his role of political adviser. The most famous and important act of Jefferson's two terms as President was the Louisiana Purchase. France owned a million square miles of territory west of the Mississippi which Napoleon was anxious to sell in order to raise money for his European wars. Paine urged Jefferson to buy, and a series of letters passed between the two men in which the whole issue was carefully discussed. Paine grew so enthusiastic about the plan that after the Purchase was made in 1803 at the bargain rate of fifteen million dollars, he thought seriously of starting a new life in New Orleans. There was a great shortage of labor and population in the new area; Paine hoped to set an example for younger men by migrating there himself. In the end, because he was sixty-six and in poor health, he gave up the idea. But his interest in the new western lands never lost its edge. When the French planters and merchants of Louisiana asked for permission to import slaves, he wrote a stinging pamphlet reminding them that the reason America had bought the territory was to spread freedom, not to strengthen slavery.

Early in 1803 Paine took his leave of the President and the capital and traveled north to his old home in Bordentown. There, in the company of Colonel Kirkbride, he settled down to a leisurely routine. He would spend each day tinkering in his workshop, writing political articles for the newspapers, and visiting the local tavern where he would drink and chat with his friends among the townspeople.

His enemies kept at him. Preachers delivered sermons against him. There were those who cursed at him when he passed in the street. Kirkbride had friends and relatives who refused even to greet Paine because of his religious opinions. On a trip to New York, Paine stopped to change coaches at Trenton, a town well known to him from the campaign of 1776. There he was jeered at by a mob that quickly gathered when word spread that Tom Paine was there. One stagecoach owner cried, "I'll be damned if he shall go in my stage." Another also refused him a seat, saying, "My stage and horses were once struck by lightning, and I don't want them to suffer again."

Finally, he hired a private carriage, but a gang of

toughs ran alongside as he left town, hooting and beating the rogue's march on a drum. The horse was scared half to death but Paine remained calm; a man who had seen the guillotine was not likely to flinch at hoodlums. In New York, however, he was guest of honor at a banquet given by the Republicans at Lovett's Hotel; a month later in Philadelphia he dined with a large group of admirers at the Franklin Hotel, where all his books except *The Age of Reason* were praised to the skies. By and large, though, many of his old friends had cooled toward him or cut him dead. The doors of many respectable houses, once open and hospitable, were now closed. All the old charges against him were revived. Again he became the target of cartoonists as well as of clergymen, and used as a bogie-man by parents to scare children. The abuse he had suffered in the days of the Revolution was mild compared to what he endured now.

In the summer of 1803 Mme. Bonneville and her three sons came over from France. Bonneville himself was not allowed to leave because of his "radical" opinions. His family arrived in America penniless and promptly threw themselves on Paine for support. It is true he had urged them to settle in America; nevertheless, he greeted their arrival with a slight sinking of the heart. He had not thought they would be entirely without money, and since he was always short of cash himself, their coming created a financial problem for him with which he struggled to the end of his life. He settled the Bonnevilles in his Bordentown house, arranged for the boys' schooling, and suggested to Mme. Bonneville that she give French lessons. Then he hurried off to his farm in New Rochelle to see what he could do about raising money.

His first plan was to sell the surplus timber on the estate, but before this could be done, he suffered an attack of the gout, an ailment made worse by a bad fall he took on the ice. These injuries compelled him to spend the winter of 1803–4 in New York City, where for a time he enjoyed the company of his Republican friends, including Mayor De Witt Clinton. He continued to contribute pieces to the press in support of Jefferson, and was overjoyed by his re-election later in the year. Mme. Bonneville was at the moment the only real fly in his ointment. Bored by life in the dull village of Bordentown, she had moved to New York and began living extravagantly. Her bills were sent to Paine for payment. When he refused to pay, he was sued, won the suit, then in a burst of generosity paid the bills anyway. He scolded Mme. Bonneville for not living within her means, but his words had little effect. She was unhappy in America. She even made little effort to learn English.

After the election Paine decided to move permanently to New Rochelle and install Mme. Bonneville as his housekeeper. In a letter to Jefferson congratulating the President on his second term, Paine described his own situation at home: "As everything of public affairs is now on a good ground, I shall do as I did after the War, remain a quiet spectator and attend now to my own affairs. . . . The farm is a pleasant and healthy situation, commanding a prospect always green and peaceable, as New Rochelle produces a great deal of grass and hay. It contains three hundred acres. . . . I have sold off sixty-one acres and a half for four thousand and twenty dollars."

But though his intentions to retire were good, his troubles continued. He was seized with a slight attack of paralysis which affected his hands and forced him to hire a man to help with the work. This man, George Derrick, turned out to be sullen and inefficient, and Paine had to fire him. Brooding over this, Derrick returned on Christmas Eve with a shotgun and fired at Paine through the window. Luckily, his aim was as sloppy and inefficient as his work. The shot missed. Derrick was arrested, but Paine refused to press charges. Still, the incident had a bad effect on his nerves.

Mme. Bonneville was no happier in New Rochelle than in Bordentown. She did not like country living and was a lazy housekeeper. Paine frequently complained about her in letters to friends, and finally packed her off in 1805 to New York, where she set herself up once again as a French tutor. Paine himself stayed on in New Rochelle where the Bonneville boys had been put in boarding school. Despite the increasing public attacks upon him, Paine continued to live on his farm in relative peace until 1806 when an incident so discouraging and humiliating to him occurred that he decided to leave his rural paradise altogether.

Paine went one day to vote in a local election. Before he could cast his ballot, he was challenged by the election supervisors, who claimed he was not an American citizen and therefore not eligible to vote. These men had been Tories during the Revolutionary War and looked upon Paine as the symbol of everything they opposed. They had gone to some trouble to look up his career in France. When Paine protested the outrage, they quoted Gouverneur Morris, who had refused to get him out of jail for the very reason they were not allowing him to cast a ballot. Paine argued violently but in vain. The man who helped found the country, who put forth proposals for universal suffrage, was now himself denied the right to vote. Made almost ill with rage, Paine could no longer endure New Rochelle. He rented the farm out and went to live in New York.

In New York he worked out his anger by sending long letters to his friends in high places, Secretary of State Madison and Vice President Clinton among others, describing what had happened and asking for justice. They sent sympathetic replies, but nothing was done. Some months later he sent a petition to Congress asking that he be paid his expenses in connection with the Laurens mission to France in 1781. "All the civilized world know that I have been of great service to the United States," ran one sentence in his letter to Congress, "and have generously given away talent that would have made me a fortune." The petition was kicked around in committees for a long while, opposed, of course, by the Federalists, and finally turned down on the grounds that Paine had joined the mission voluntarily and was not officially appointed, and that he had kept no itemized list of his expenses and therefore it was impossible to verify his claim.

In the sixty-ninth year of his life, Paine was a cruelly hurt and disappointed old man. That his body was failing disturbed him less than the blows and rebuffs which his spirit and pride had received. Even the company of his friends in New York, with whom he took long walks through the parks and along the river front, did not console him. Such energy as he had left, however, continued to pour into letters and pamphlets. He wrote a long account of yellow fever, bombarded the newspapers with statements on the issues of the day, and lashed back at his enemies. He even thought again of moving to Louisiana.

For a time he lived as a guest in the home of John Wesley Jarvis, the sculptor, who did a famous bust of Paine. In Jarvis' house he was seized one day with a fit of apoplexy which for the moment paralyzed him. "I had neither pulse nor breathing," he wrote to a friend, "and the people about me supposed me dead. I had felt exceedingly well that day, and had just taken a slice of bread and butter for supper, and was going to bed. The fit took me on the stairs, as suddenly as if I had been shot through the head; and I got so very much hurt by the fall, that I have not been able to get in and out of bed since that day . . . Yet all this while my mental faculties have remained as perfect as I ever enjoyed them. I consider the scene I have just passed through as the equivalent of dying, and I find death has no terrors for me . . ."

He recovered from this seizure, left Jarvis, and took up lodgings on his own. He had become increasingly careless of his physical appearance and grew more untidy every day. He spent long hours in working-class taverns with a glass of brandy before him, staring into space in a kind of daydream. "Old Tom Paine" he was called by young and old alike, and became something of an institution in the life of the city.

Occasionally, he would rouse himself under the spur of some political crisis. The British had resumed their war with Napoleon, again were stopping neutral American ships on the high seas and forcibly impressing American sailors into their navy. Protests from the capital were ignored, and the public temper began to rise as a series of such incidents occurred. Finally, in the summer of 1807, the British warship *Leopard* fired at the American frigate *Chesapeake*, killing three of its crew and wounding eighteen.

LAST YEARS

There was a great outcry in America and much talk of war. Jefferson was furious, all the more so because his sympathies were naturally pro-French. Paine wrote a series of articles for the New York *Public Advertiser* on the subject of whether war would be declared. The war fever passed, however, and in December an embargo was declared by the government, preventing ships from leaving for foreign ports until freedom of the seas was assured. Five years later, the War of 1812 broke out, in part because of the continued kidnaping of American sailors by England, but by that time Paine was dead and Jefferson no longer President.

In 1808 Paine's fortunes and health sank steadily. After moving from one unsatisfactory lodging to another, he finally rented a room in the house of a Mr. Ryder in Greenwich Village. The Village in those days was a small hamlet in rough country two miles removed from New York City, which meant that some of Paine's friends found it difficult to visit him. Irritations of one kind or another cropped up. A man named Fraser published a book in which Paine was reported as taking back the opinions expressed in *The Age of Reason*. Hailed into court, Fraser pleaded poverty as the excuse for his libel. When Paine was satisfied that this was true, he let the matter drop.

He was pestered by clergymen of various sects and by pious women who came to beg him to repent. He asked the Ryders not to admit them, or if they should break in, to be present in his room. He wanted witnesses to testify that he had not changed his mind. "My opinions are before the world, and all have had an opportunity to refute them if they can; I believe them unanswerable truths, and . . . I do not wish to argue on the subject." For the most part, however, he was quite alone.

At the beginning of 1809 his loneliness grew worse. He had formed no close ties with the Ryder family, who were becoming alarmed by his failing health. He lost his appetite, had more and more frequent seizures, could no longer move about by himself, and became increasingly irritable and hard to live with. He kept begging Mme. Bonneville to visit him. "I am here all alone, for all these people are nothing to me, day after day, week after week, month after month, and you don't come to see me." She did come to see him, bringing her sons. At Paine's insistence, she rented a house nearby to which she moved him, resolved to nurse him as best she could. But she could see that the end was not far off.

Two years before, he had drawn up a will, leaving his property to the Bonnevilles and requesting that he be buried in a Quaker cemetery. But he was afraid that the Quakers would refuse. If that happened, he wished to be buried on his New Rochelle farm. The last sentence of his will read: "I have lived an honest and useful life to mankind; my time has been spent in doing good; and I die in perfect composure and resignation to the will of my Creator, God." With this serene statement he made his peace with the world and prepared himself for death.

Though ready for death, he hung on to life with his last ounce of energy. In the spring of 1809 his body became swollen with dropsy but he pleaded with Mme. Bonneville to read the newspapers to him every day. She had caused him much irritation and grief earlier with her extravagance and irresponsibility, but she more than made up for it in her faithful care of him during these final months when he was scarcely able to move. As news of his mortal illness spread, the house was bombarded by curiosity seekers, scandalmongers, the religious faithful who wanted Paine to repent, and a small handful of old friends who loved the dying old patriot for his own sake. To these visitors, Paine remained alert and responsive. He was no longer in control of his body, but his mind remained clear and unclouded to the end.

The effects of dropsy were made worse by a mysterious digestive disturbance which made it harder and harder for the ailing man to hold his food. While his limbs swelled, his frame grew thinner and more wasted, and the struggle for breath became more painful. He spoke his last words to Mme. Bonneville on the night of June 7. The next morning, after a final restless night in which he was heard to groan aloud in the grip of some agitating dream, he died—and one of the great careers of the eighteenth century came to its final end.

The Quakers refused burial, as Paine had feared. So on June 9, the funeral procession made its way slowly over the twenty-mile route to New Rochelle. The procession included the body of Paine, on which Mme. Bonneville had placed a rose; the Frenchwoman and her three sons; Willett Hicks, a Quaker friend of the dead man; and two unidentified Negroes. At the corner of the farm which Paine had selected as his burial place, a number of passersby attracted by the ceremony had gathered. Mme. Bonneville placed her son Benjamin at one end of the grave and herself at the other. As the coffin was lowered into it, she cried: "Oh, Mr. Paine, my son stands here as testimony of the gratitude of America, and I, for France!" A week later she carried out his last wish, erecting a tombstone on which were inscribed the words mainly written by Paine himself: "Thomas Paine, Author of Common Sense, died the eighth of June, 1809, aged 72 years."

But even in death he was not left in peace. Vandals sliced off branches of the trees around the grave and chipped out pieces of the tombstone as souvenirs. Ten years later, in 1819, occurred one of the strangest of all events. William Cobbett, an English reformer who had fallen under the spell of Paine's ideas, dug the coffin up one night with the help of two hired men, and transported it to England. His plan was to exhibit it in various cities, and thereby raise money to carry out Paine's reforms, a mission which Cobbett felt himself to have inherited. The English government refused to grant permission for this weird scheme, and in the wrangle that followed, Paine's body disappeared altogether after returning, symbolically as it were, to the country of his birth. "As to his bones," commented M. D. Conway, Paine's first biographer, "no man knows the place of their rest to this day. His principles rest not. His thoughts, untraceable like his dust, are blown about the world which he held in his heart."

In a way this was a fitting end for Tom Paine, who regarded all of humanity as his country and thought of himself as a universal man. When still young, he had enrolled under the banner of freedom and remained its loyal and energetic apostle to his last day. In its name he had helped create one country, the United States, played a large role in the life of another, France, and left his deep mark on still a third, England. Without formal education, without benefit of family connections, he had won in his lifetime enduring fame, notoriety and influence. He had stirred the hearts and shaken the minds of his contemporaries as few men did, and carved for himself a permanent place in the annals of history.

His faith in reason and the power of reason to solve

human problems was one of the great dreams of his time. After a century and a half, it remains one of man's great dreams, made all the brighter and more meaningful because Tom Paine lived.

INDEX

Adam, Robert, 61

Adams, John, 130, 157, 170-171, 190

Adams, Samuel, 9, 192

Addison, Joseph, 5

Age of Reason, The, 150-159, 201; storm aroused by, 156

Agrarian Justice, 174

Aitken, Robert, 20, 24

Alien and Sedition Laws, 185

America, Paine's arrival in, 15-21; vision of, 21; Paine leaves, 111; Paine returns to, 186-189

American Revolution, 2; *Common Sense* as immediate cause of, 31; end of, 98-99; history of, 52-53; motivation for, 9; people's attitude toward, 23-24; role of Paine, 33-34, 74

Amiens, Treaty of, 184

Appeal from the New to the Old Whigs, 131

atheism, charge of, 6, 150, 156

attacks on Paine, 6, 32-33, 135-138, 156-157, 189-195, 198

Babeuf, François, 174

Bache, Richard, 16, 19, 34

bankers: defended by Paine, 108-109; support from, 39

Banks, Sir Joseph, 112

Barlow, Joel, 151

Bastille, storming of, 115-116

Beaumarchais, Pierre Augustin de, 42-43

Bien Informé, Le, 181, 182

biography by Chalmers, 129

Bible, Paine's attack on, 152, 192

Blake, William, 126, 141

Bonneville, Mme. Nicholas, 182, 195-197, 202, 203, 204

Bonneville, Nicholas, 127-128, 173, 181-183

Bonneville family, 181-182, 195, 202

Bordentown, Pa., 194; first bridge models by Paine, 103

Boston Tea Party, 192

Brandywine, Battle of, 75, 81

bridge, iron, Paine's interest in, 99-114, 125, 176-177, 188-189

bridges, 18th century, 101

Brissot (de Warville), Jacques, 127, 145

British Army, 7, 13

British rule in Colonies, 9

bullets, rationing of, 10

INDEX

INDEX

INDEX

ABOUT THE AUTHOR

Leo Gurko is professor of English at Hunter College in New York and served as chairman of the department from 1954 to 1960. Educated at the College of the City of Detroit and the University of Wisconsin, he is the author of *The Angry Decade; Heroes, Highbrows and the Popular Mind;* and *Joseph Conrad: Giant in Exile.*

At various times Dr. Gurko has worked as advertising copy writer, translator, free-lance editor, and publisher's reader. He has made frequent appearances on radio and television, and has written many articles on modern English and American literature.

A year in Europe with his family in 1953–1954 was made possible by a grant from the Ford Foundation. While there he did research in Paris and London for *Tom Paine, Freedom's Apostle.*

Among his avocations are tennis, travel, baroque music, and professional baseball. He and his wife, herself an author of biographies for younger readers, live in New York. They have a son and daughter.

92
PAI
GURKO, LEO
Tom Paine

10095